Ms. Muffintop's

Fantasy Sweetheart Collection Vol. 2

Fauns, Mermaids, and More

Adult Coloring Book

Dear Customer,
 Thank you!!!! For purchasing my book! What a great feeling to have a Volume 2 of my Fantasy Sweethearts! I can't believe I've made it this far! Thank you for joining me on my journey of life as an artist. The best is yet to come.

LOVE XOXO's
Ms. Muffintop

Upon enterning the world of Ms. Muffintop...

* This book is made for coloring!
* The pages can take heavy coloring, BUT put a safety sheet behind the page that you are coloring. Just in case!
*2 copies of each coloring page. 50 pages total!
*Single page use
*color test pages

Ms. Muffintop's

Color Test Page!!!

Test your colors here!

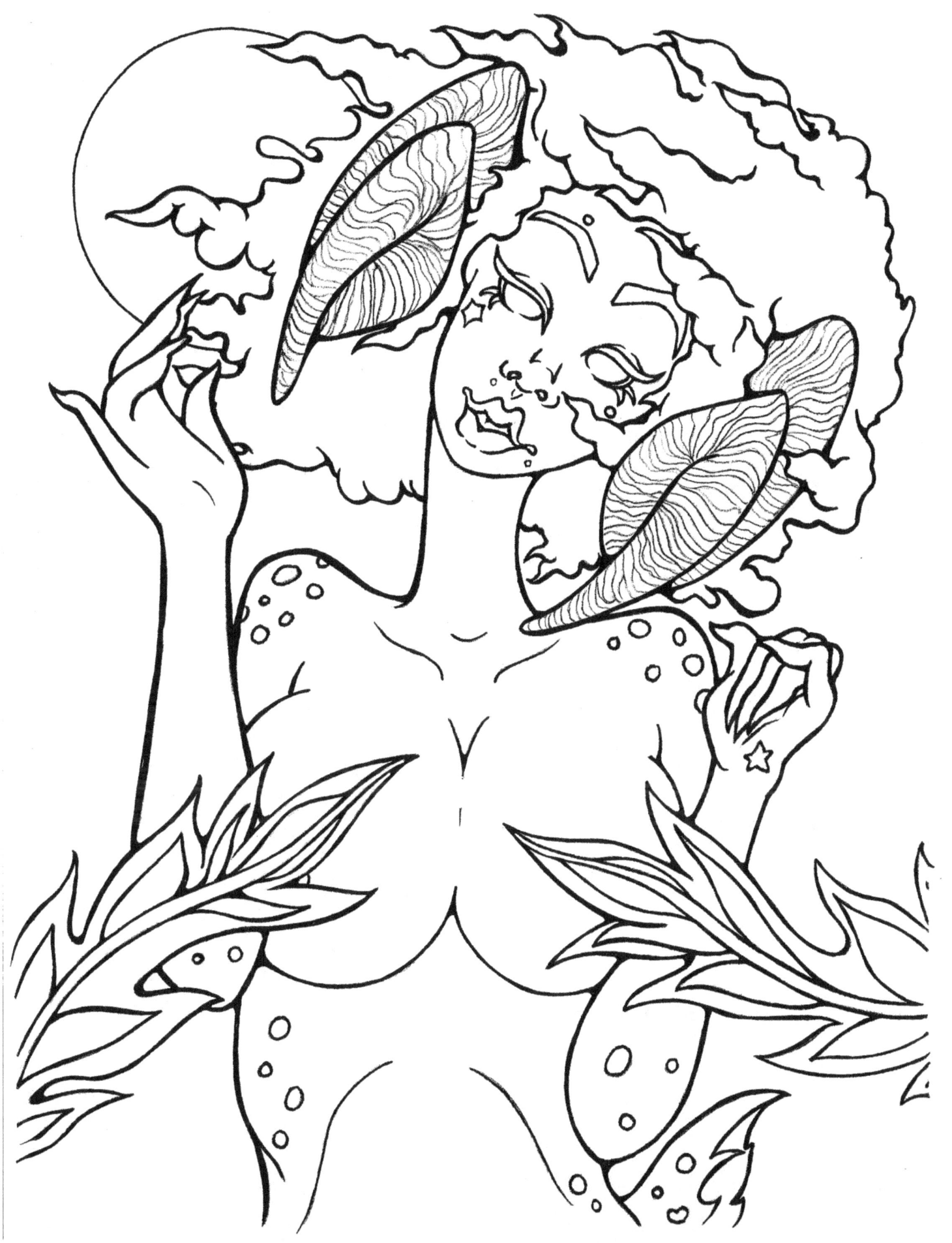

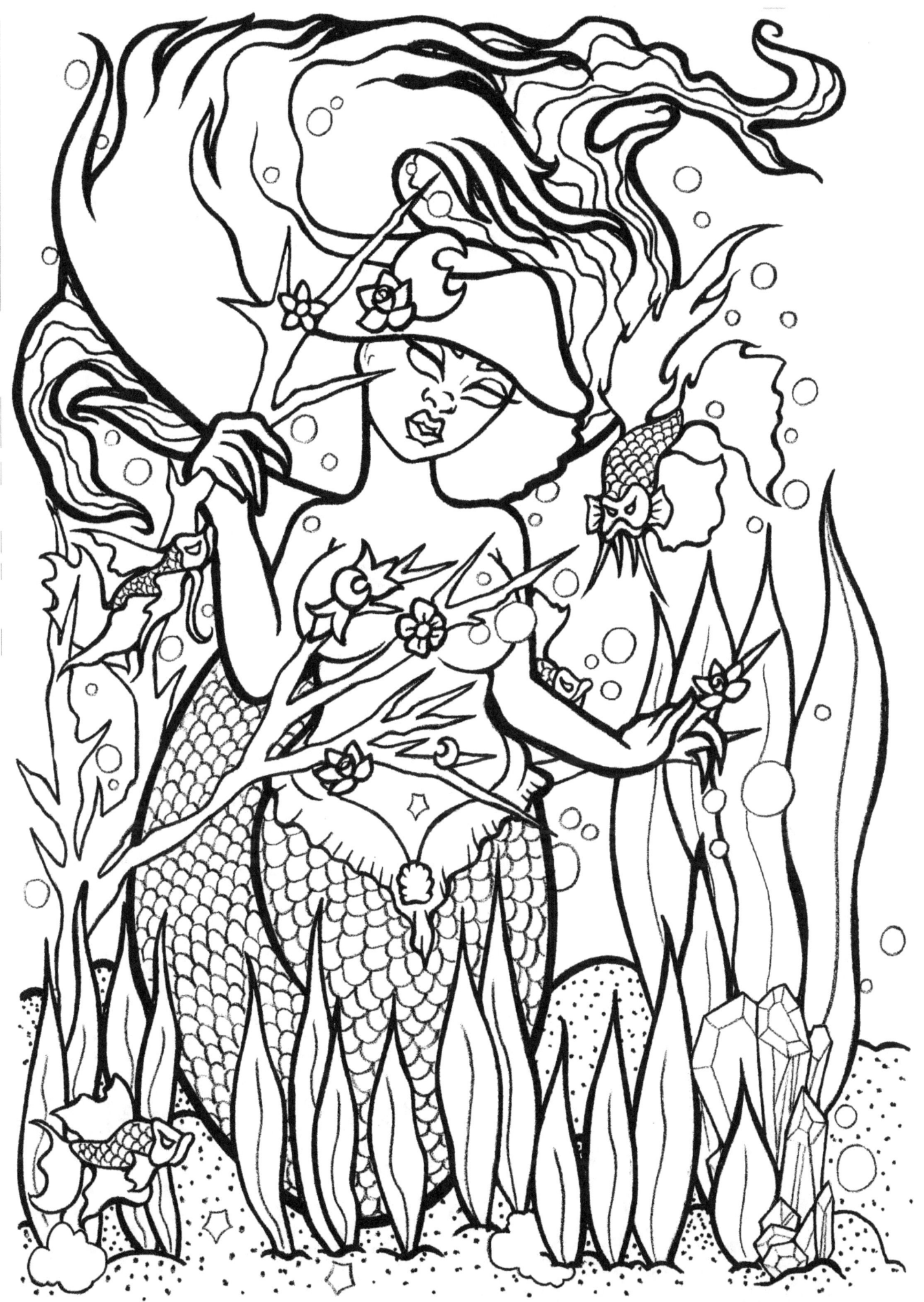

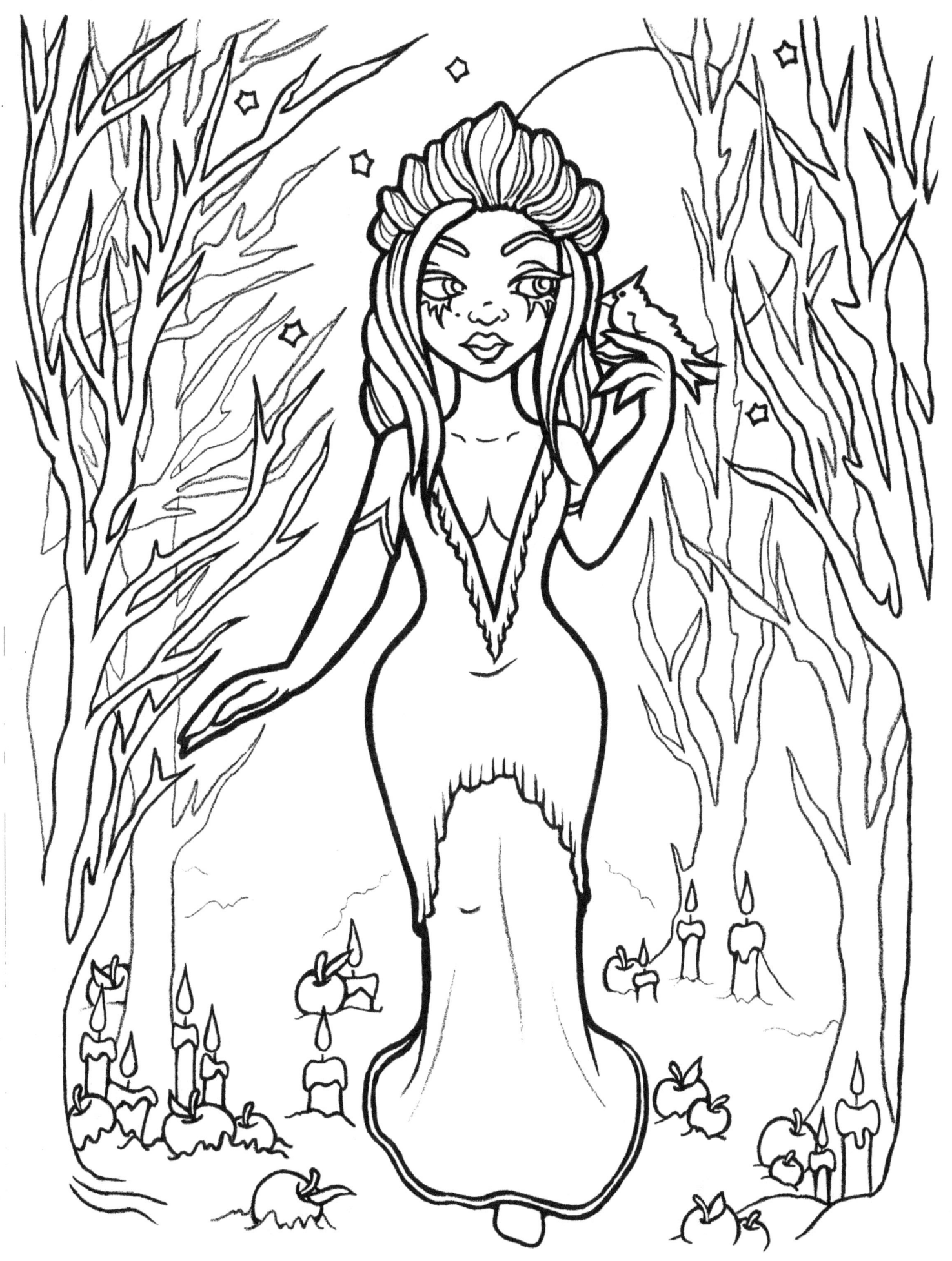

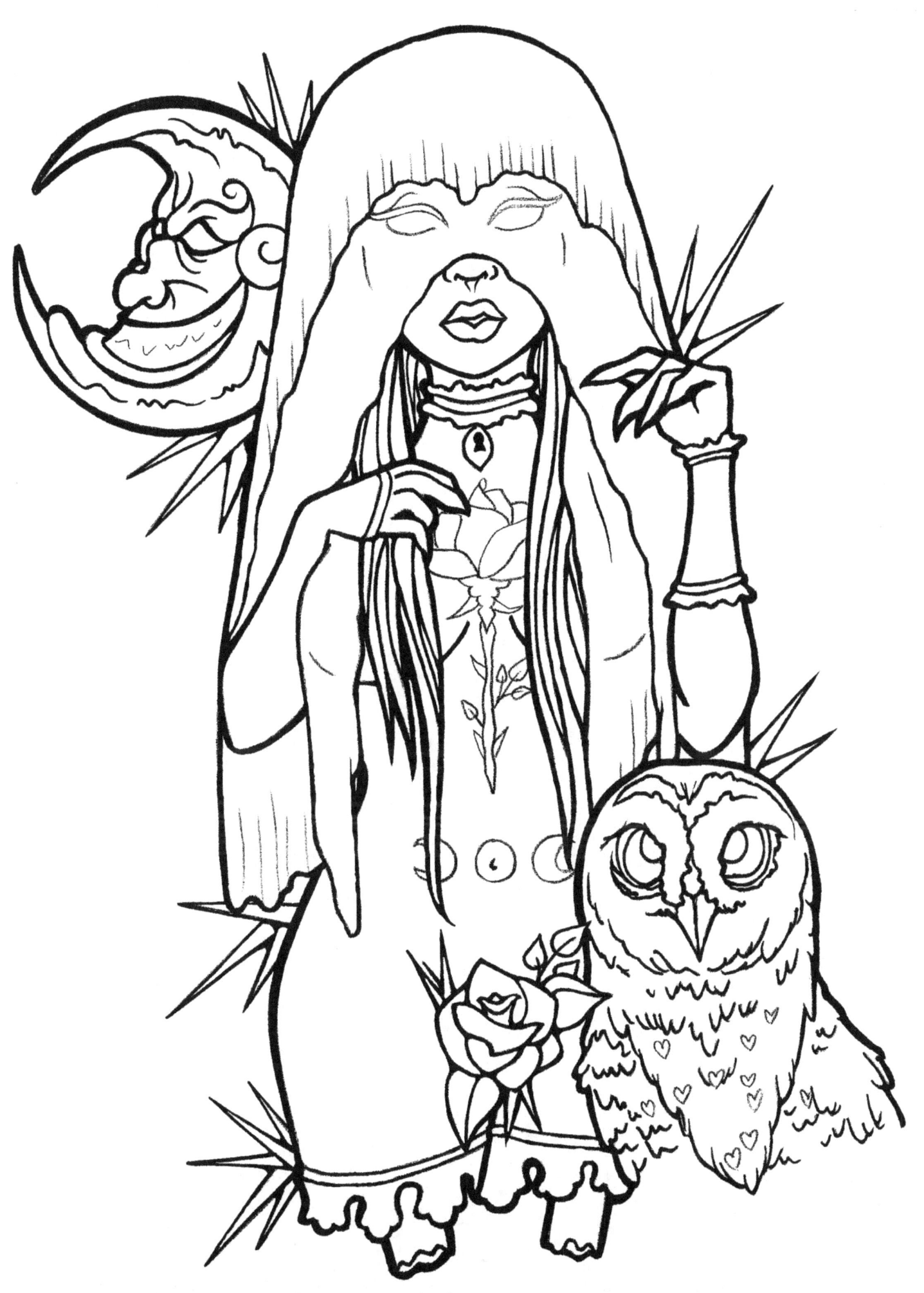

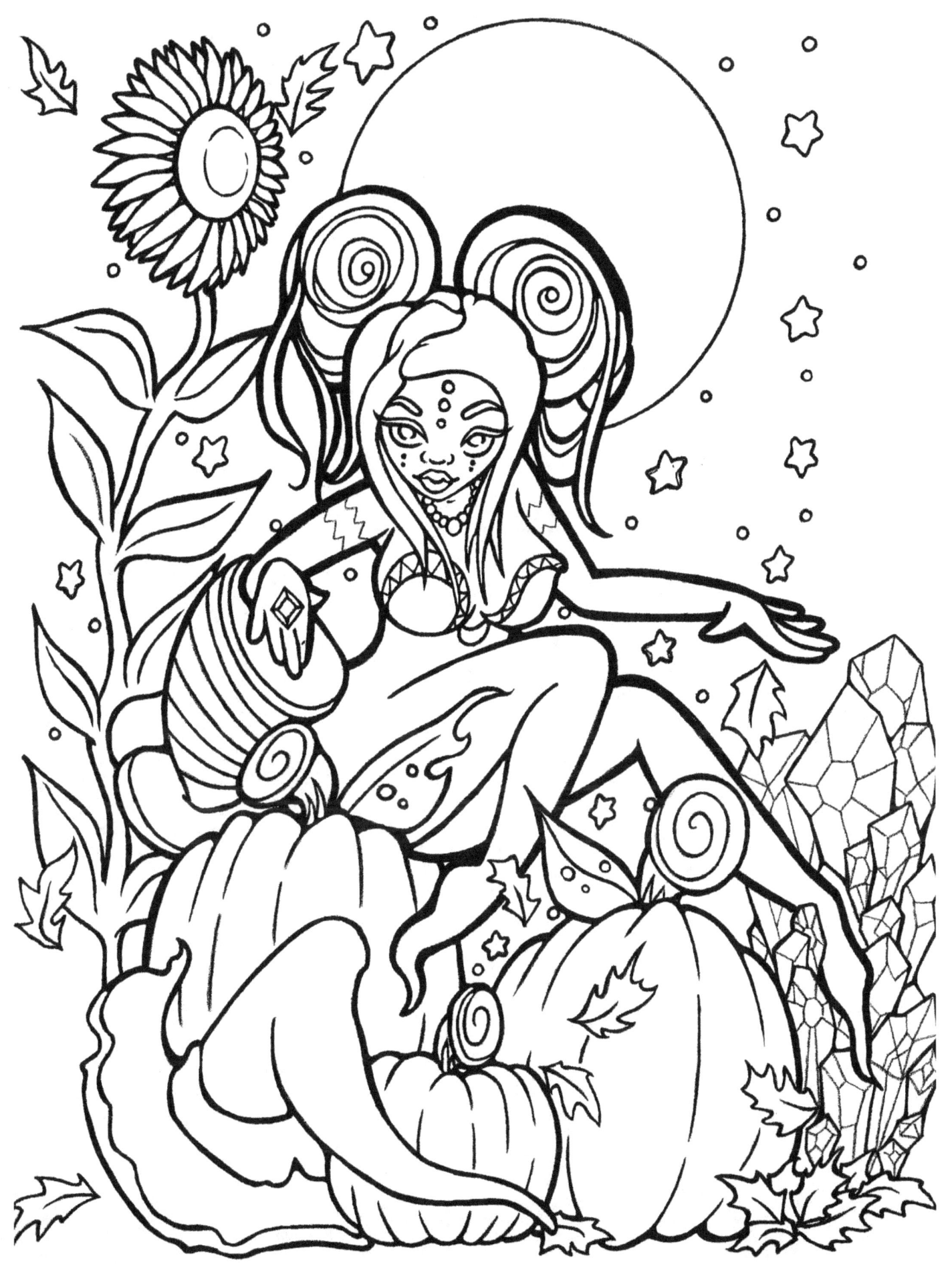

Ms. Muffintop's

Color Test Page!!!

Test your colors here!

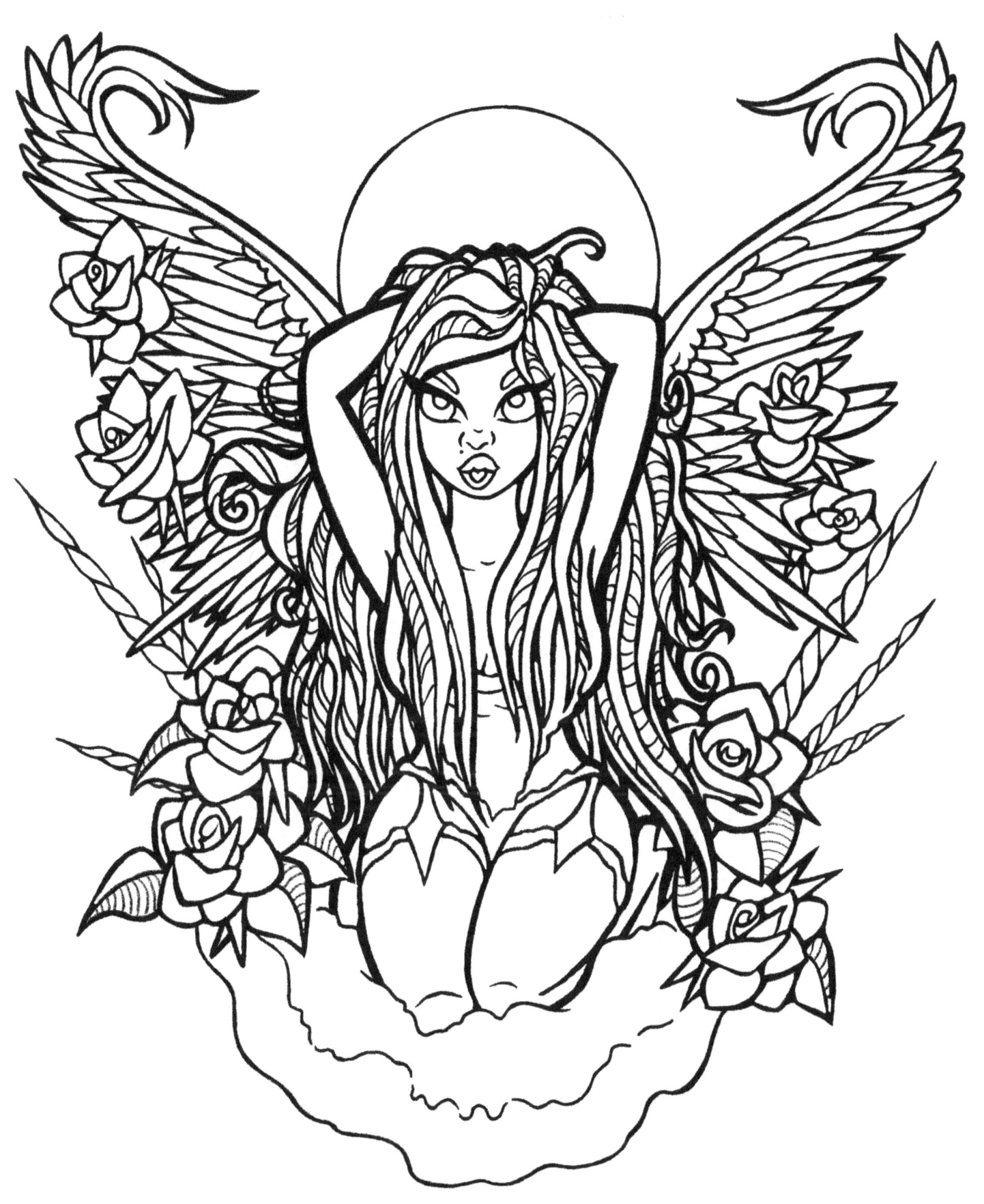

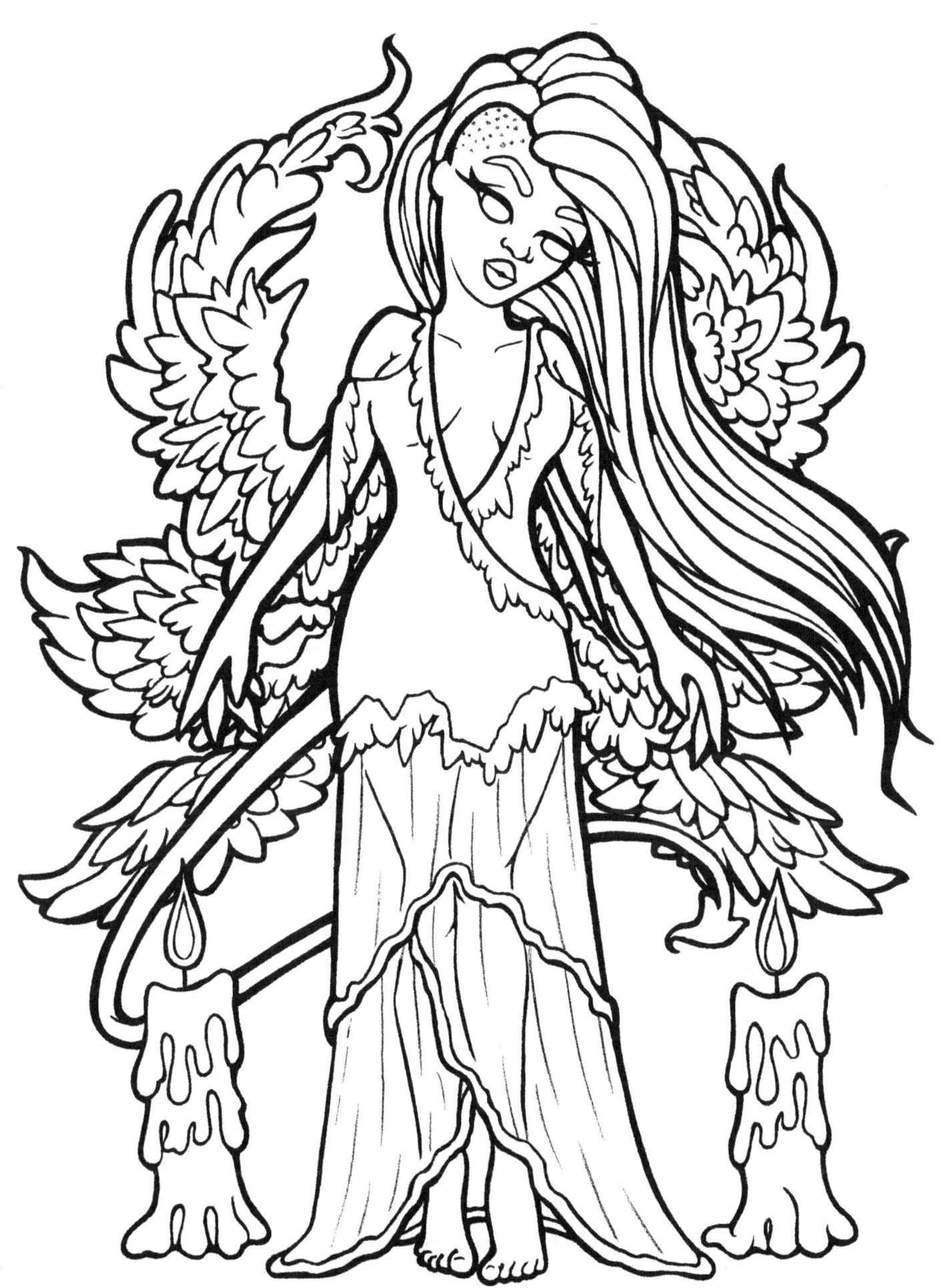

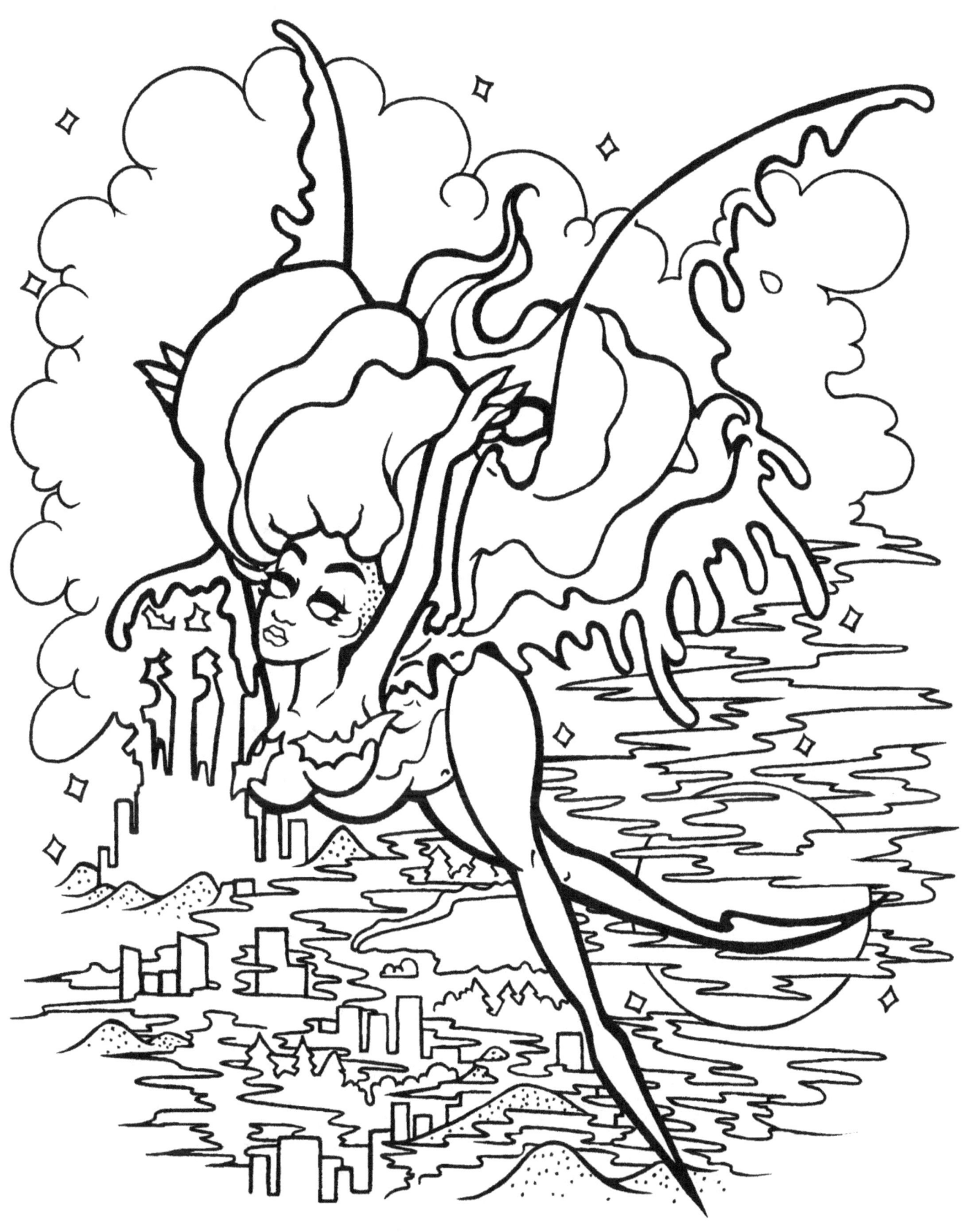

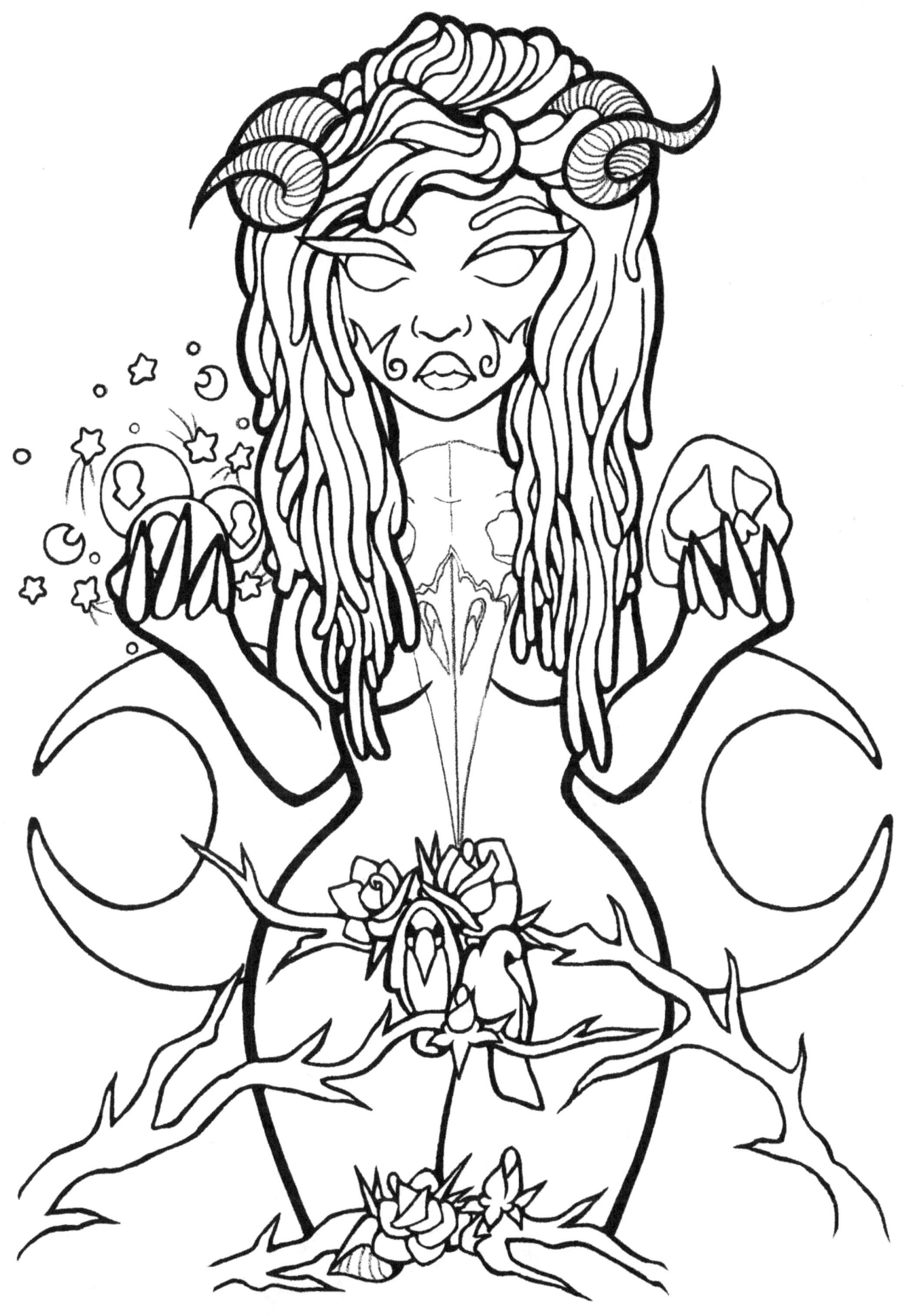

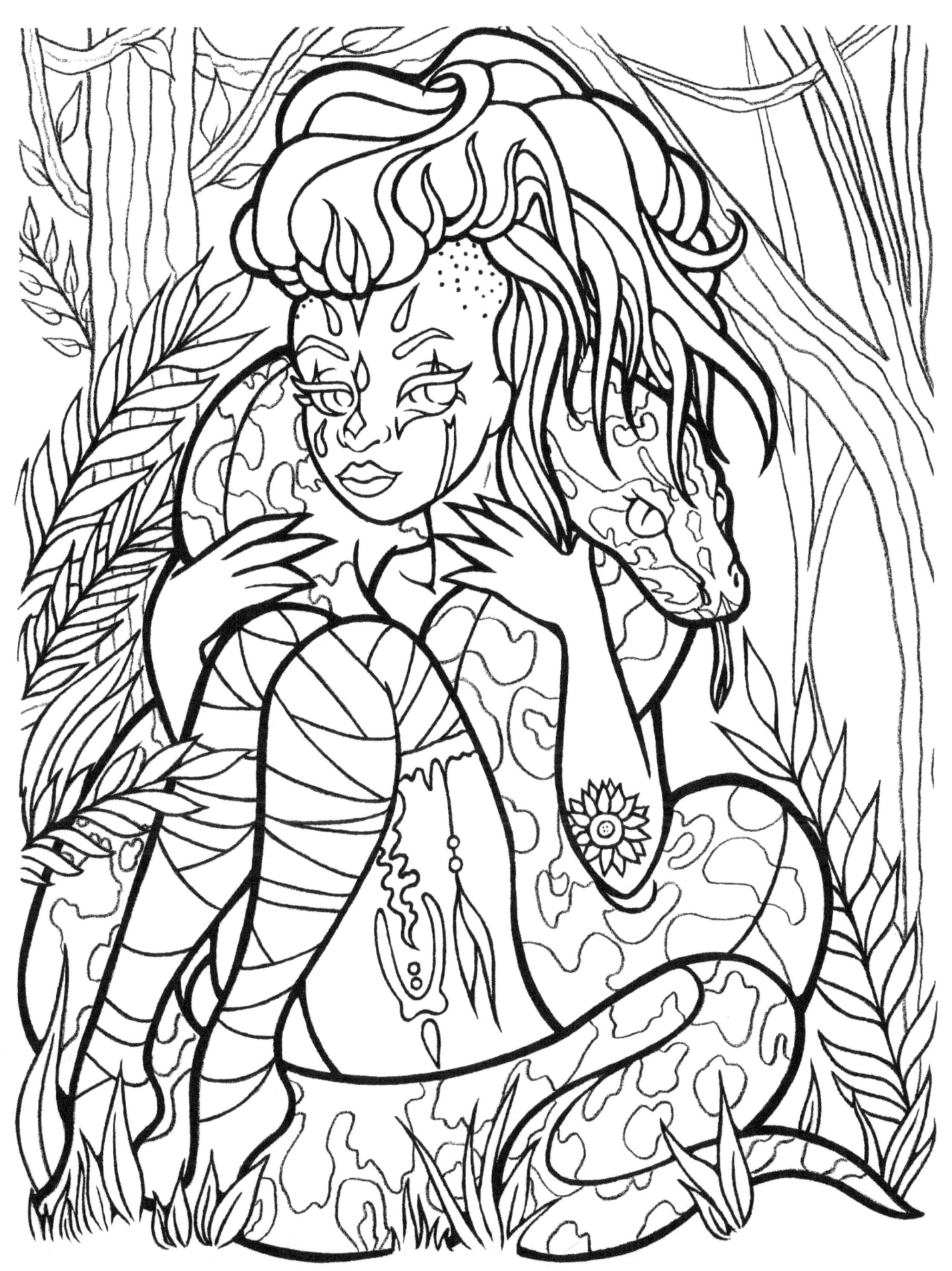

Ms. Muffintop's

Color Test Page!!!

Test your colors here!

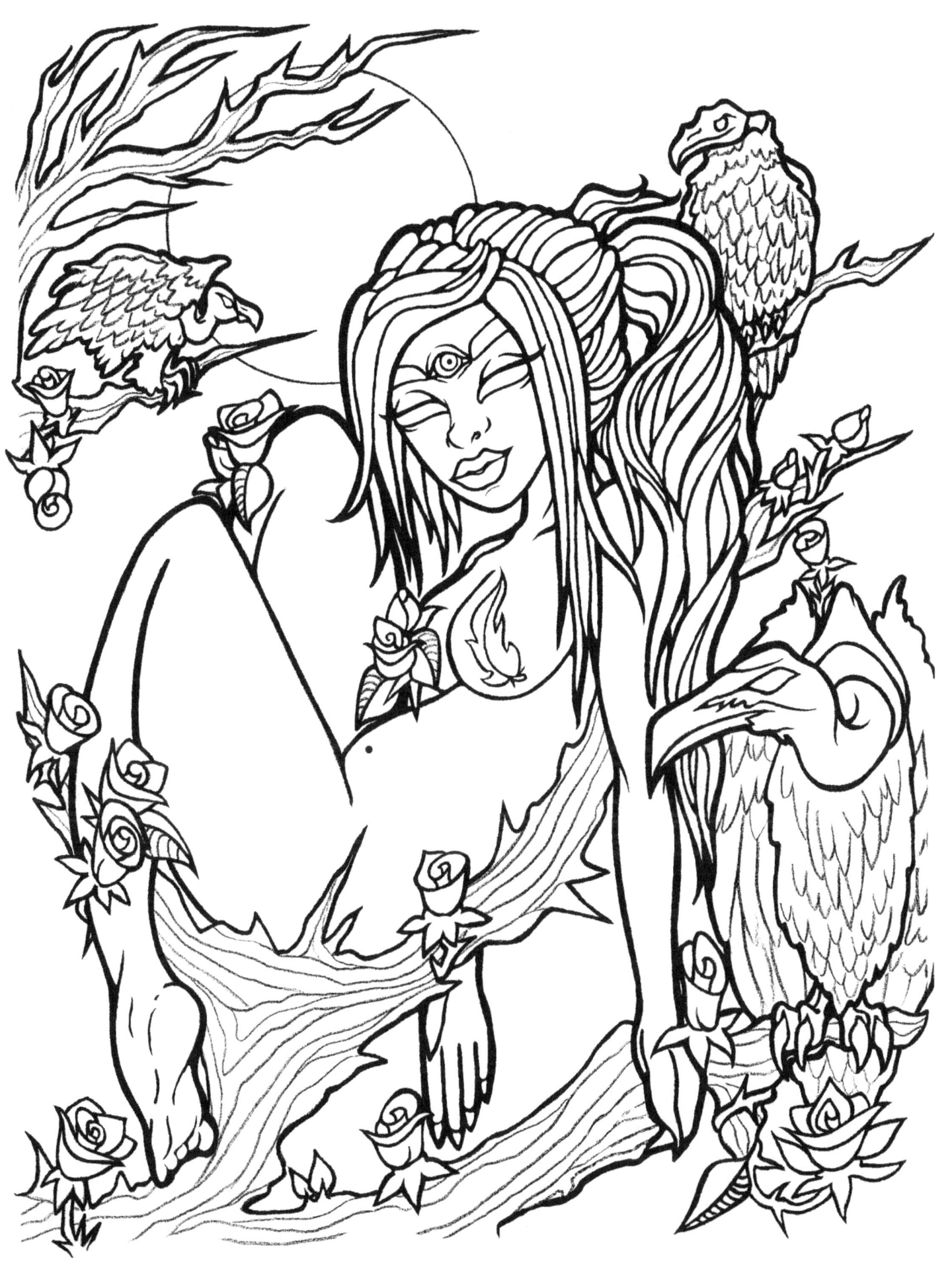

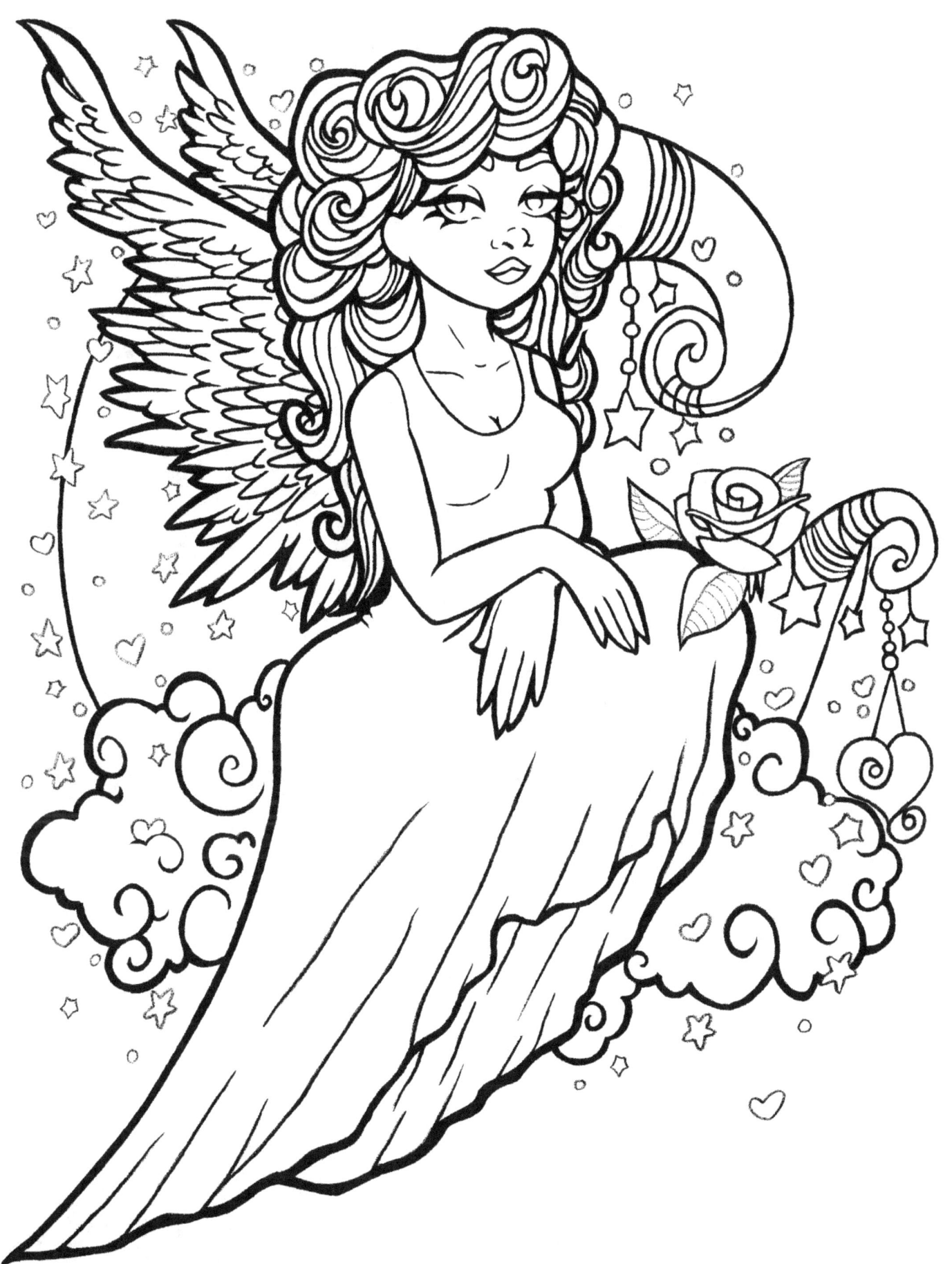

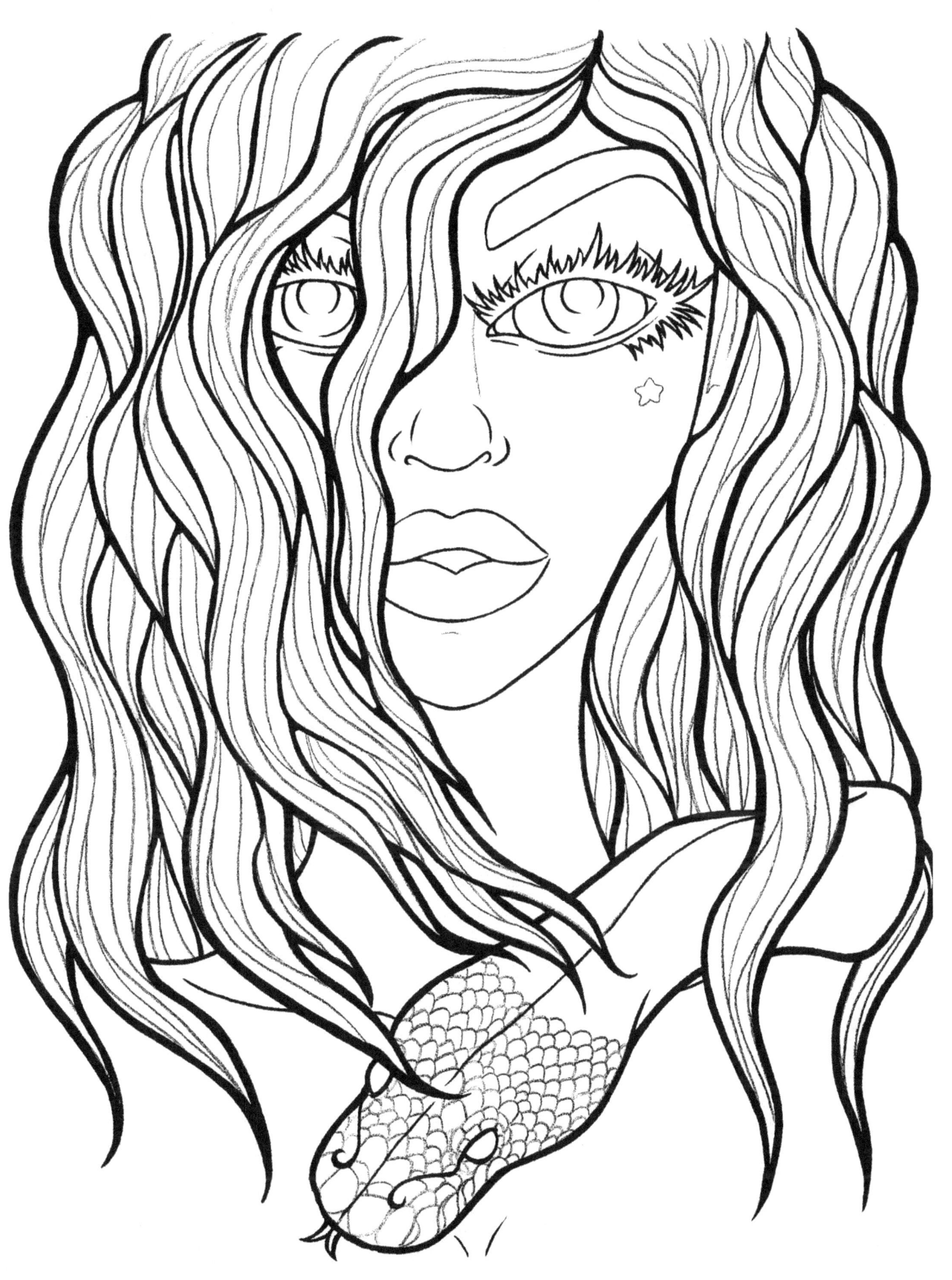

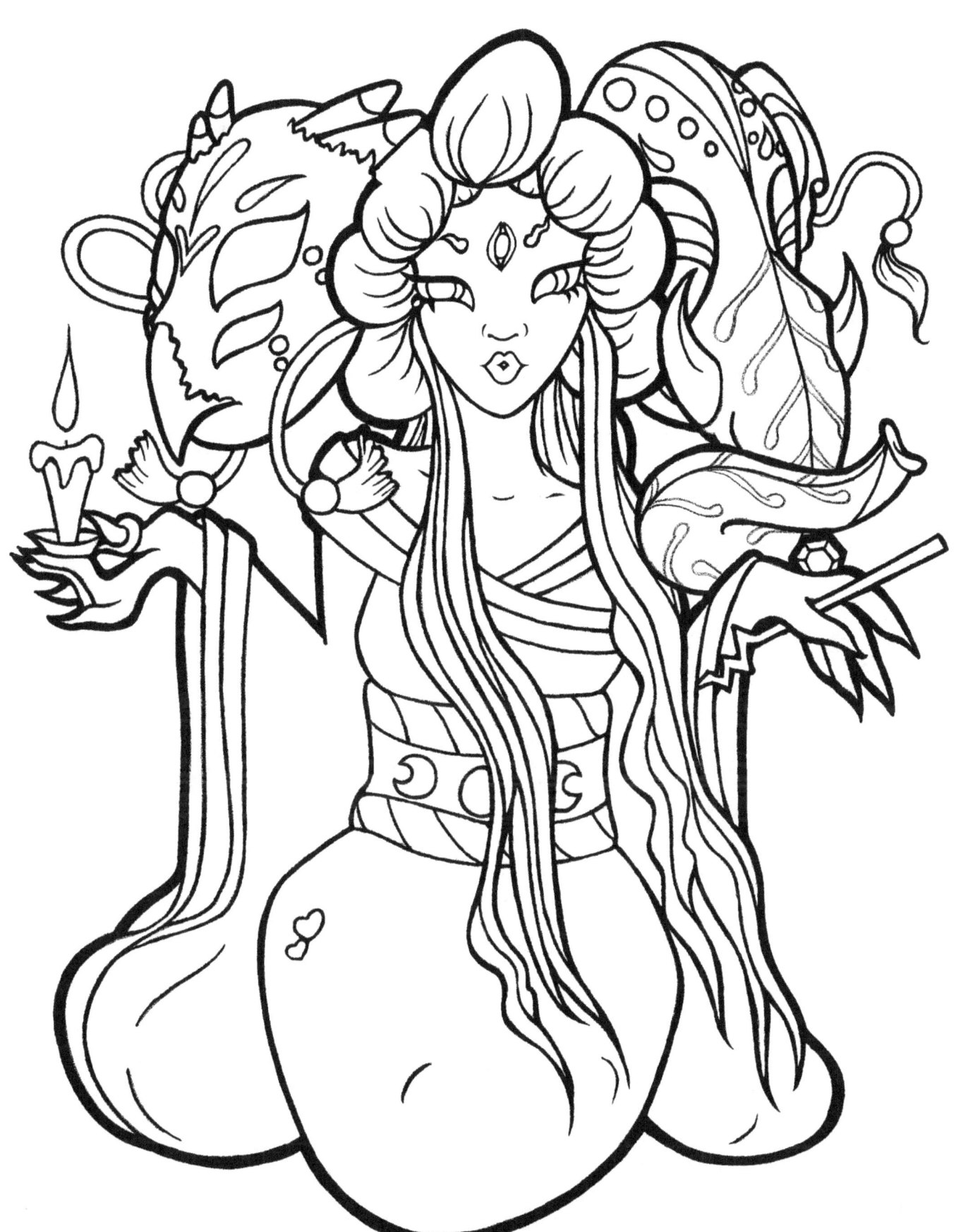

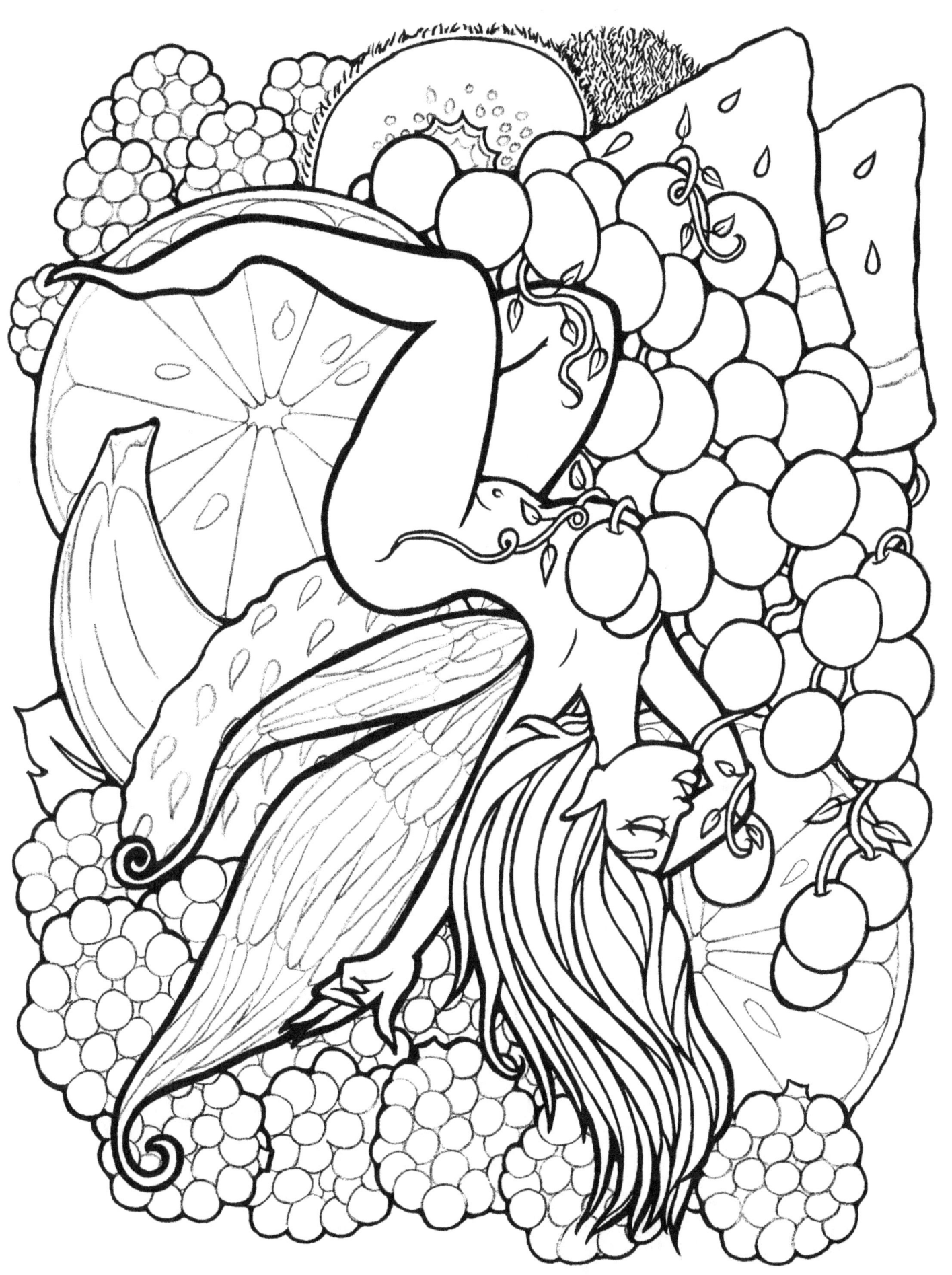

Ms. Muffintop's

Color Test Page!!!

Test your colors here!

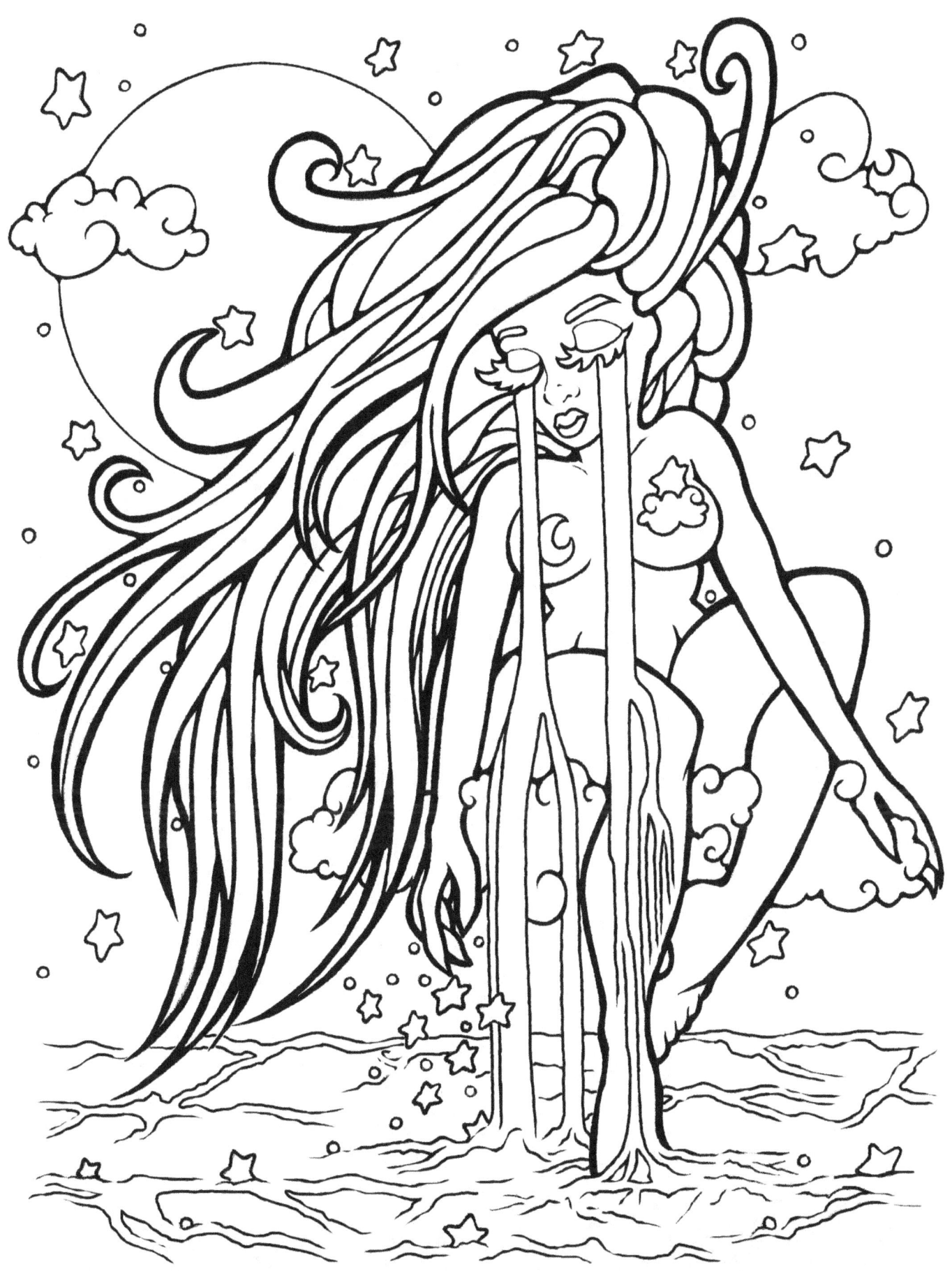

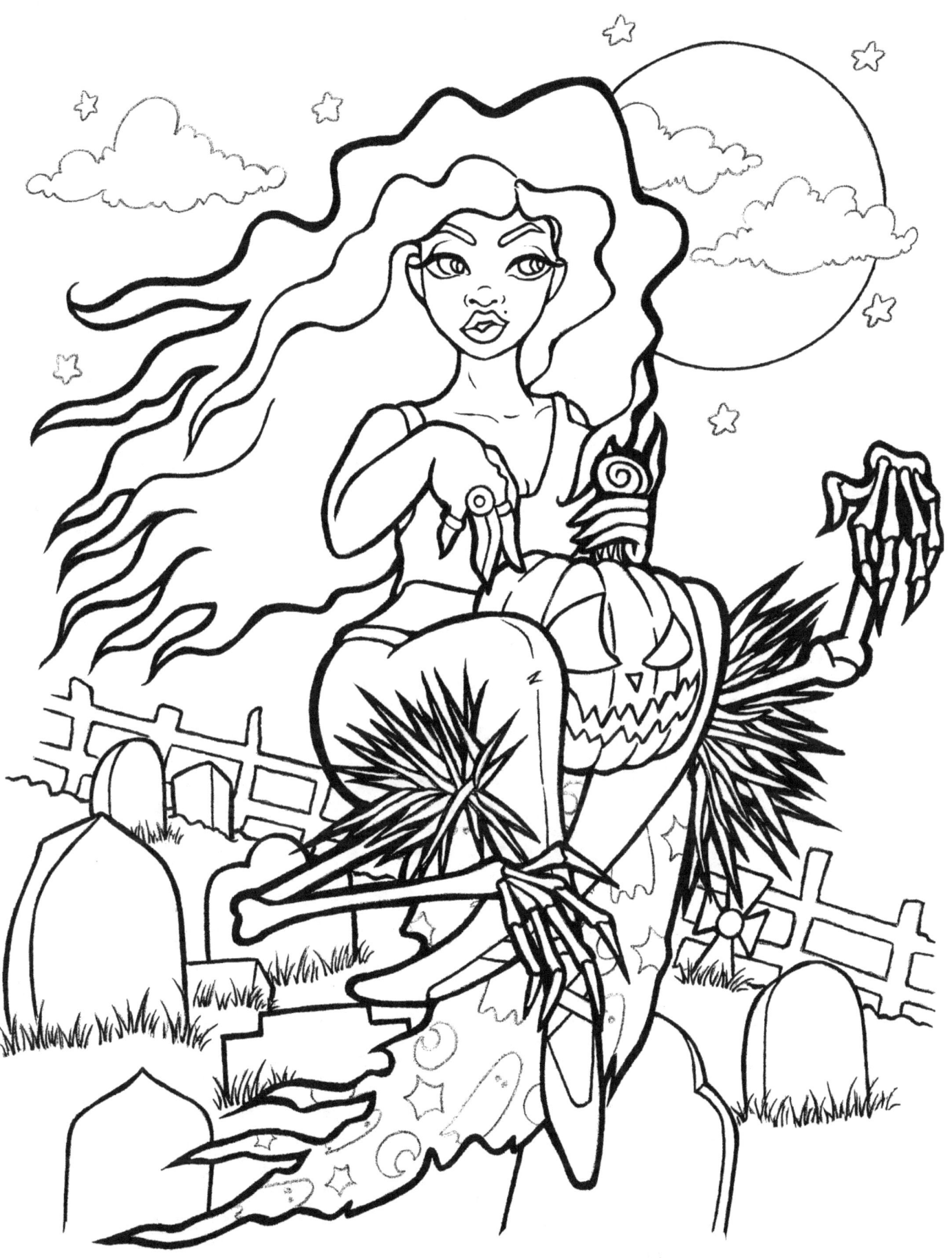

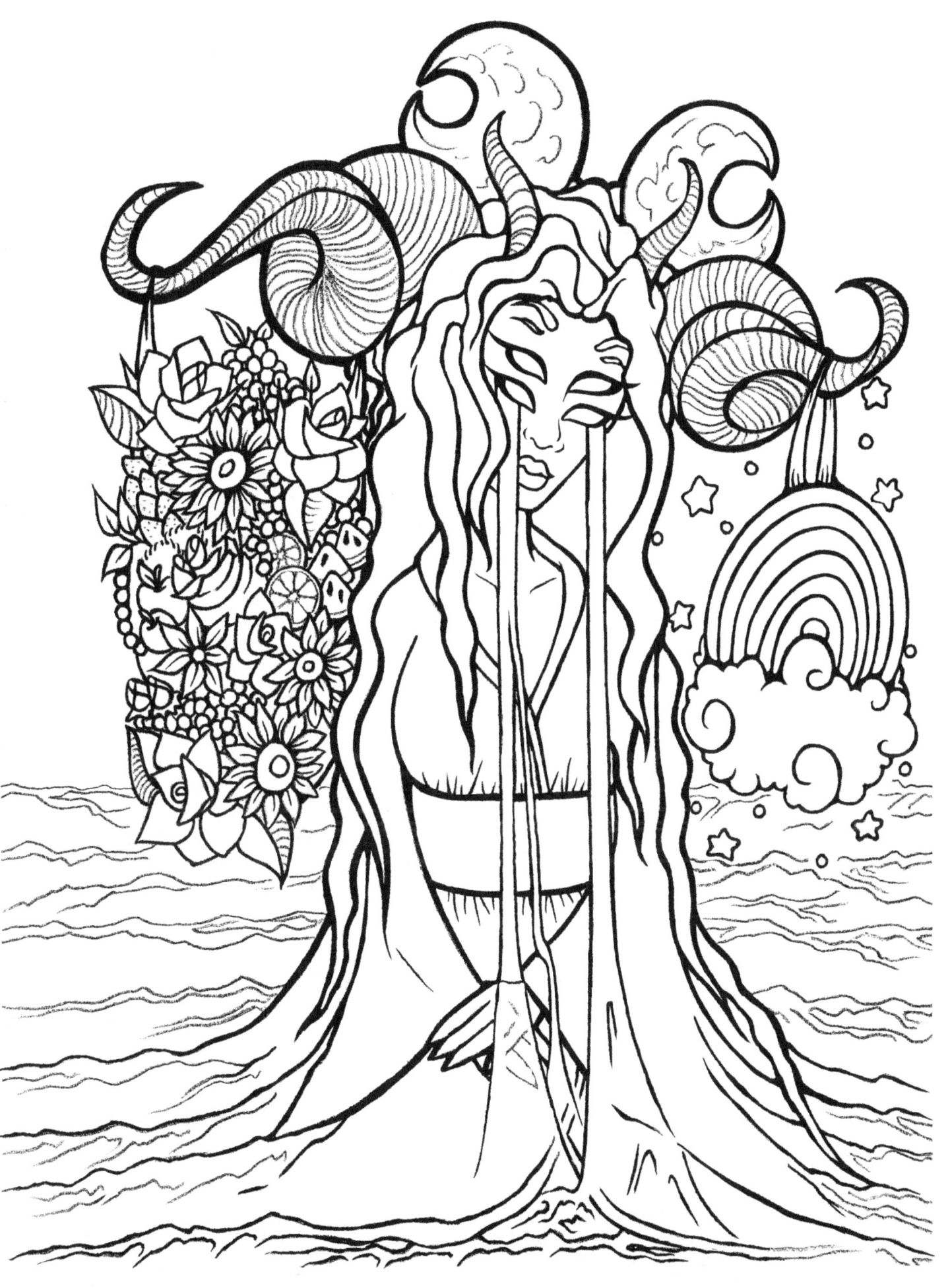

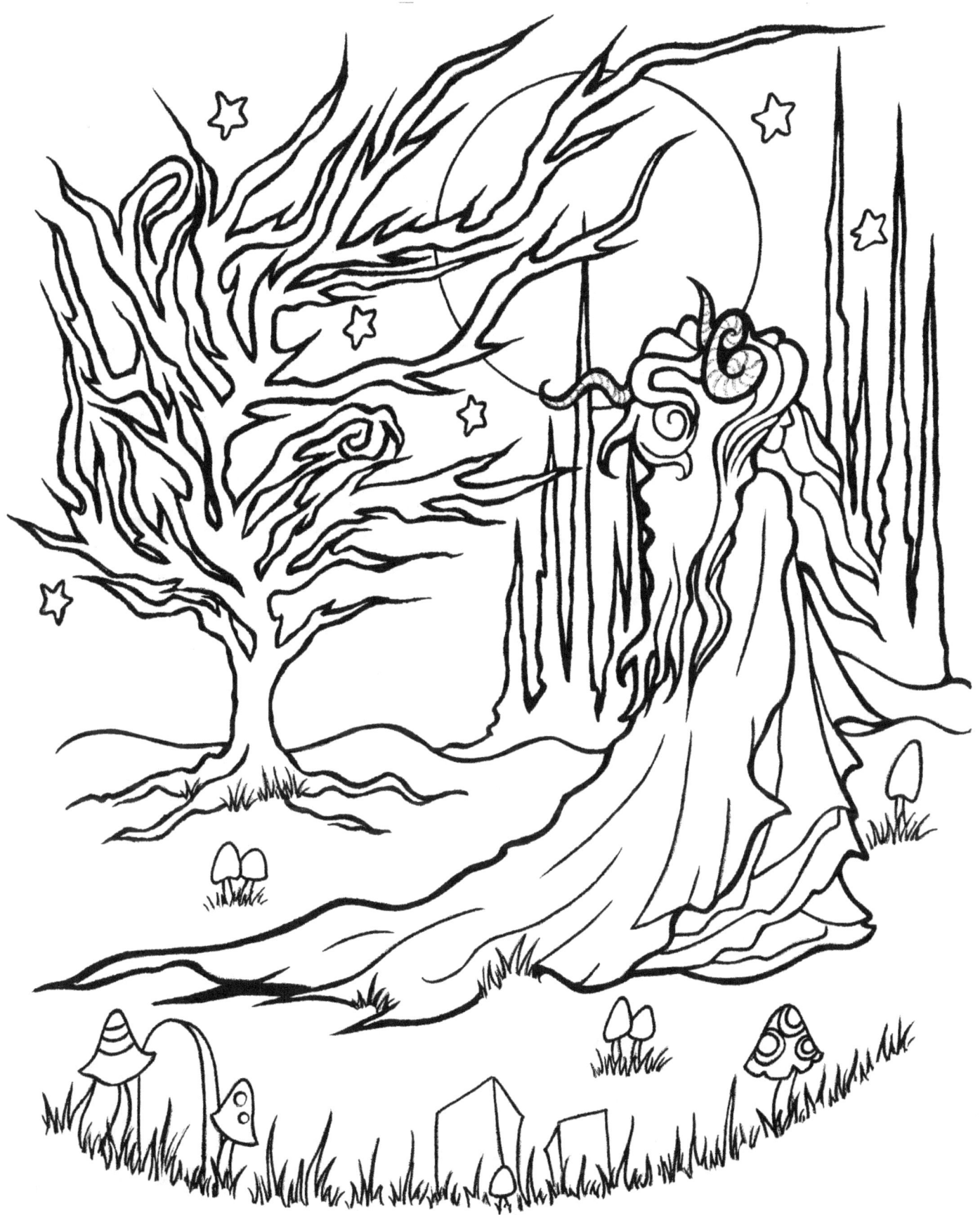

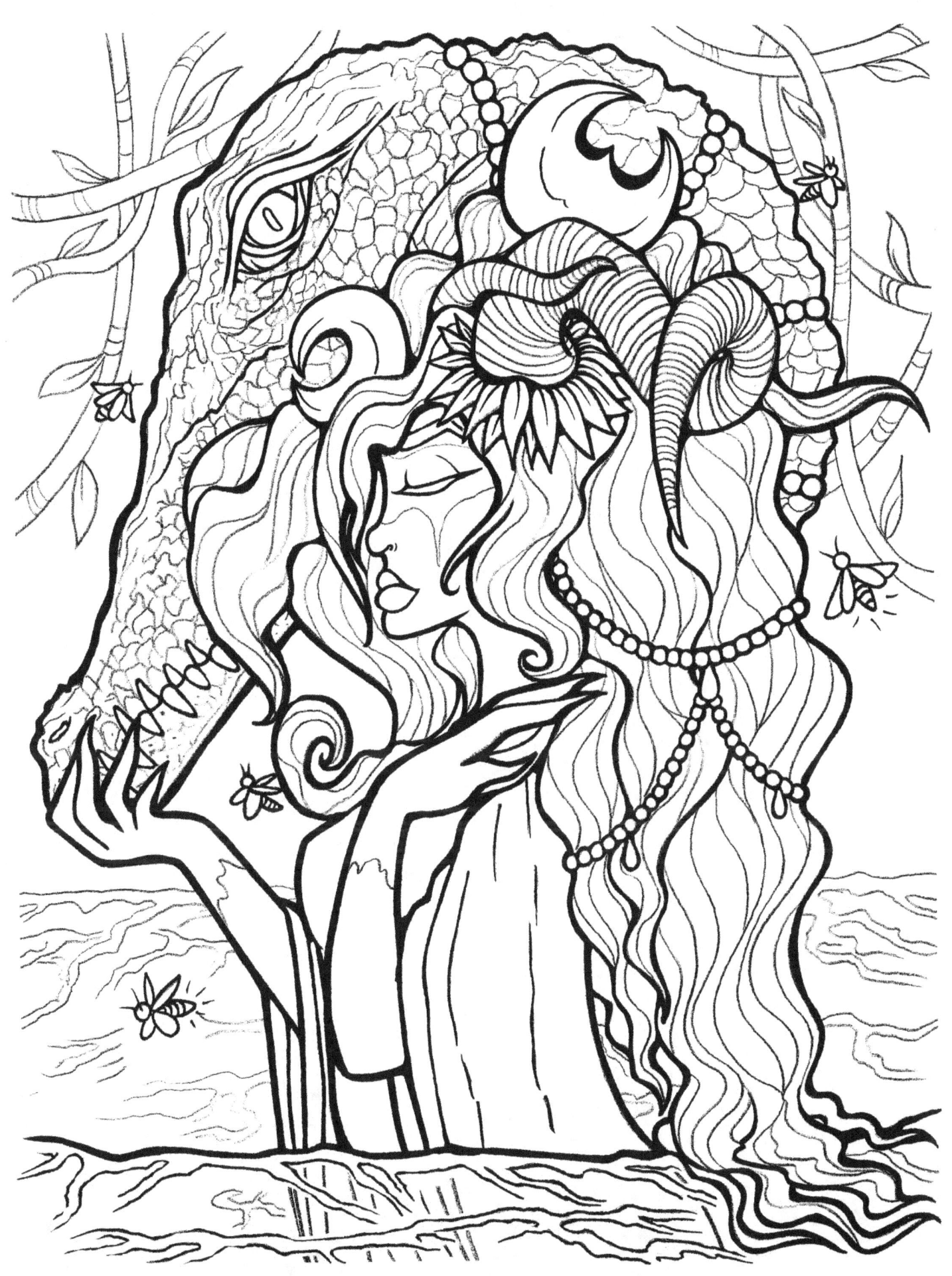

Ms. Muffintop's

Color Test Page!!!

Test your colors here!

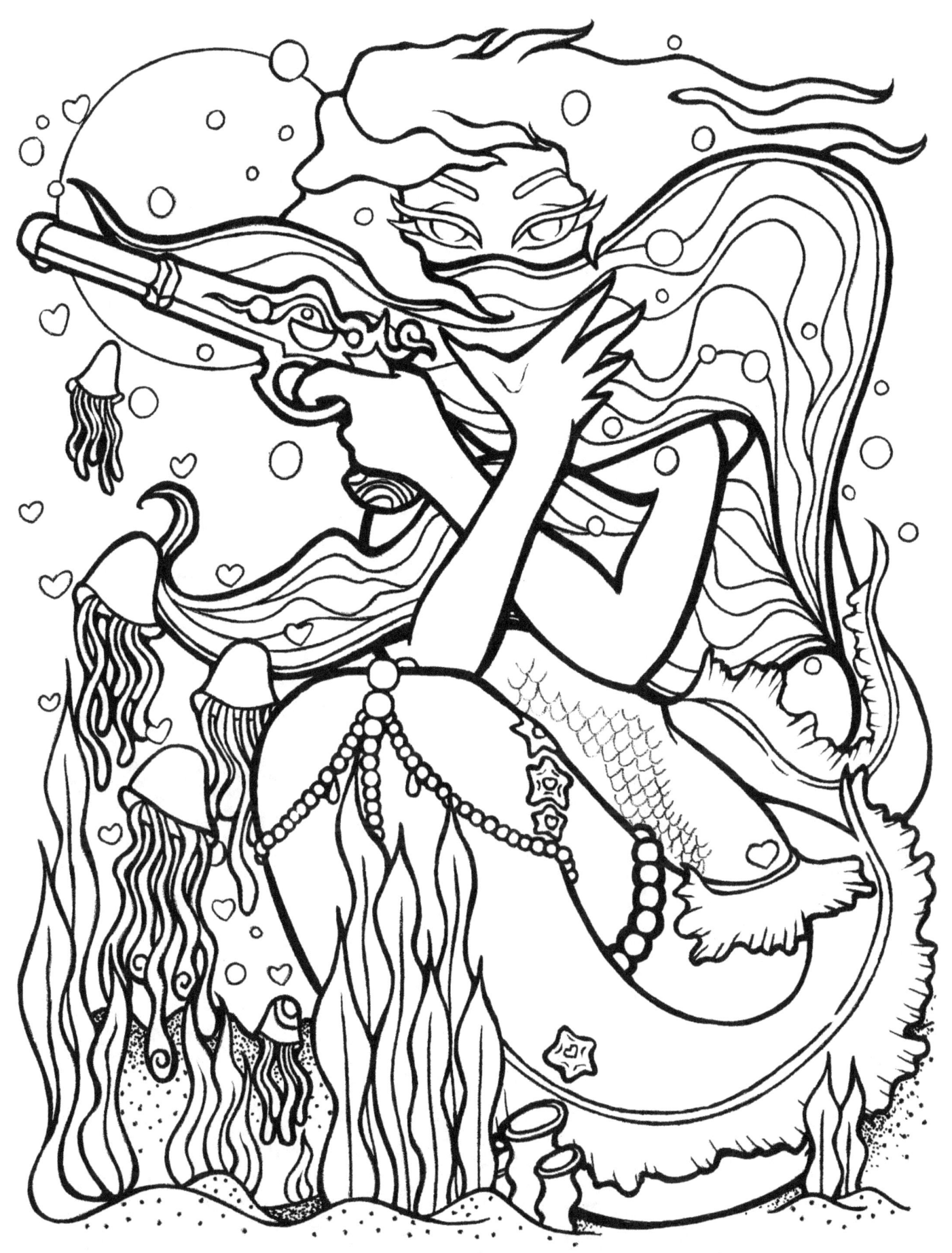

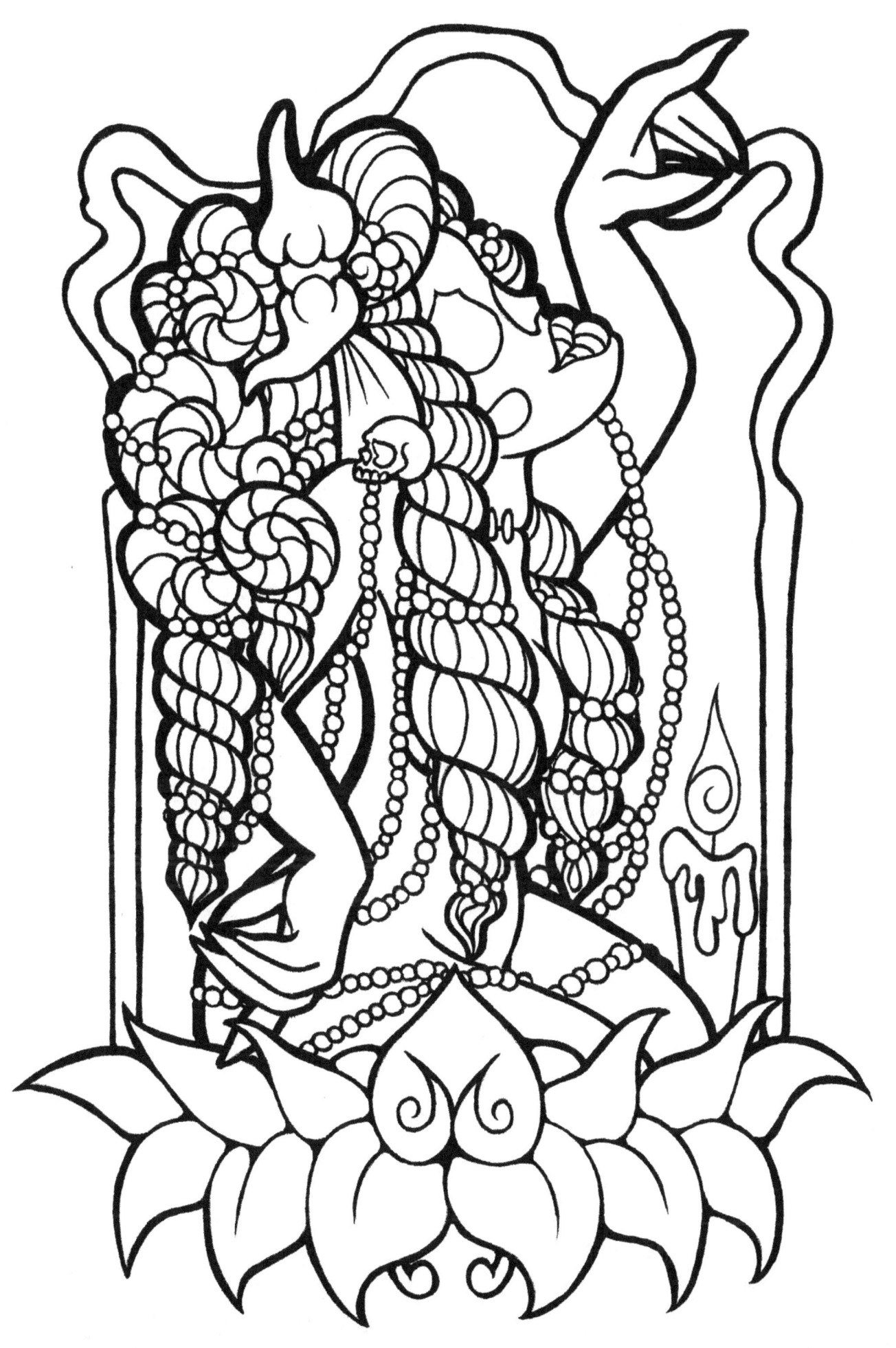

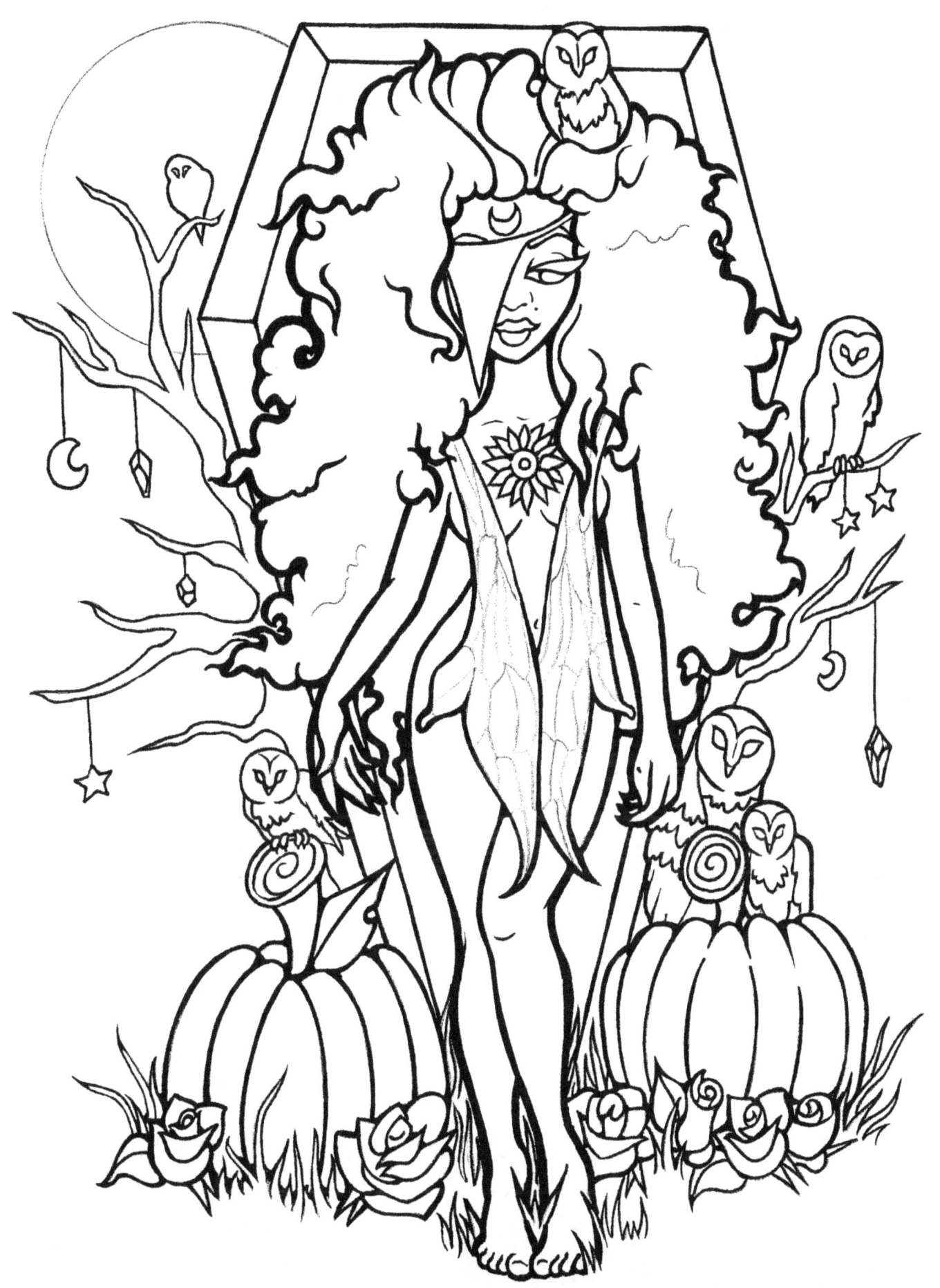

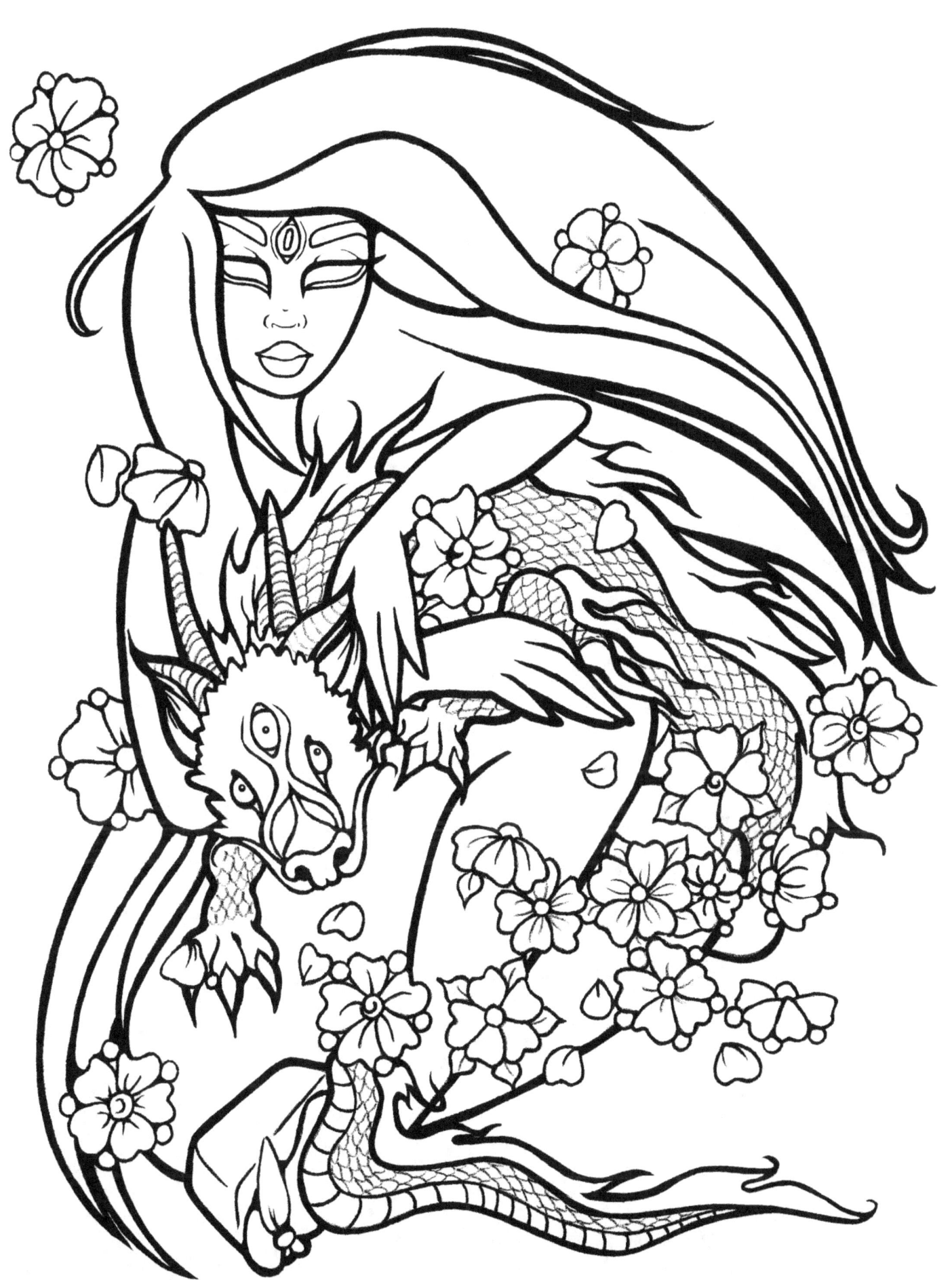

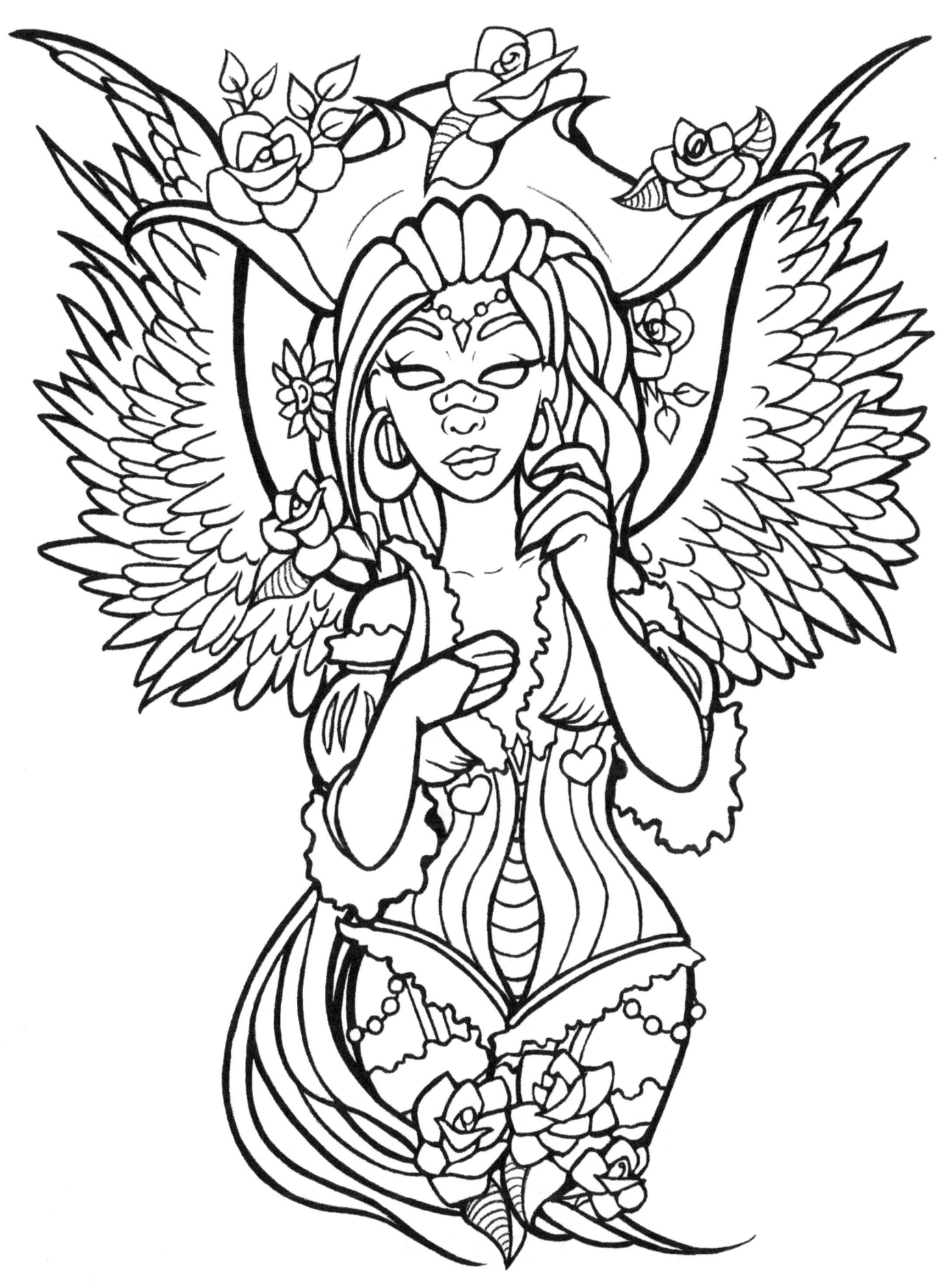

Ms. Muffintop's

Color Test Page!!!

Test your colors here!

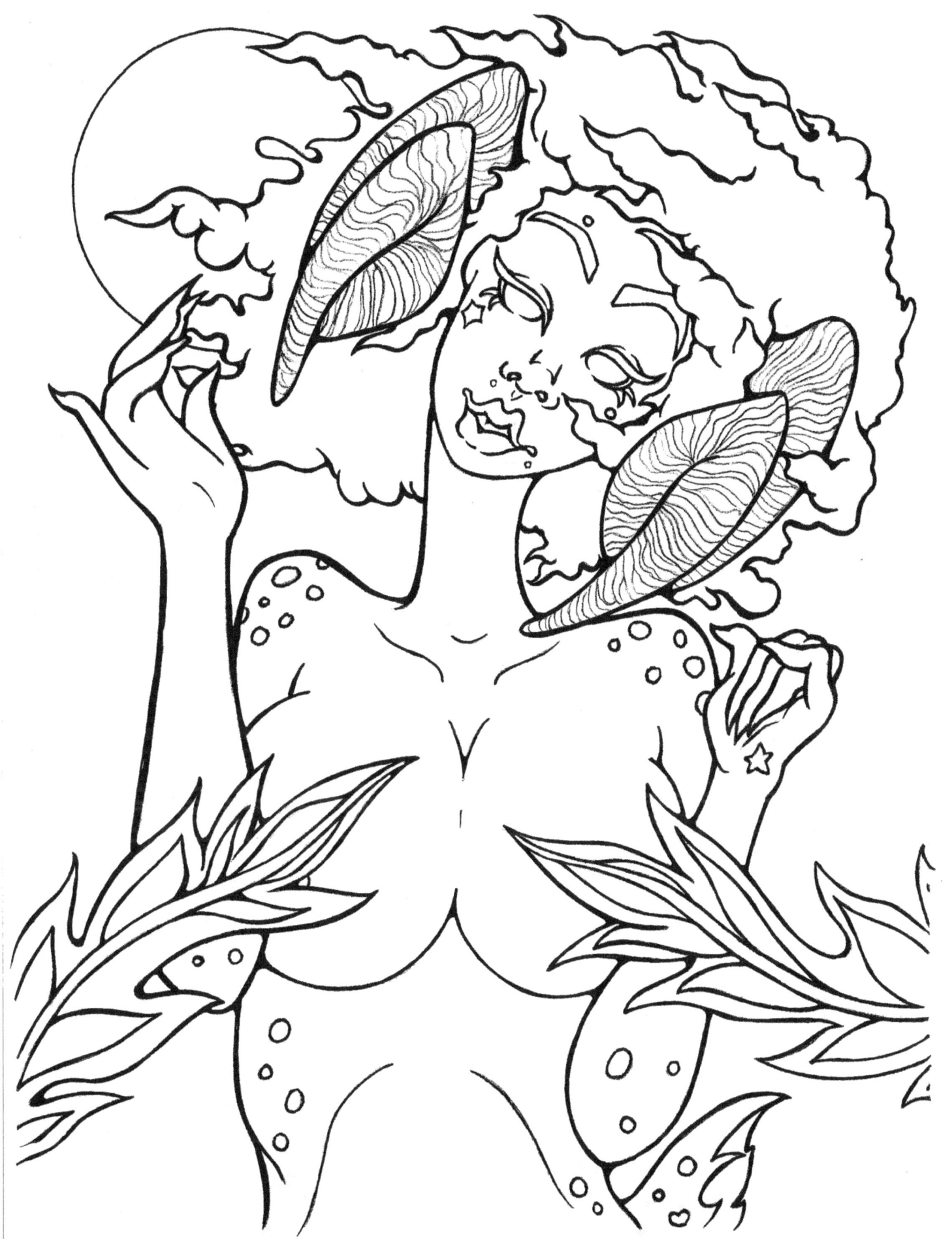

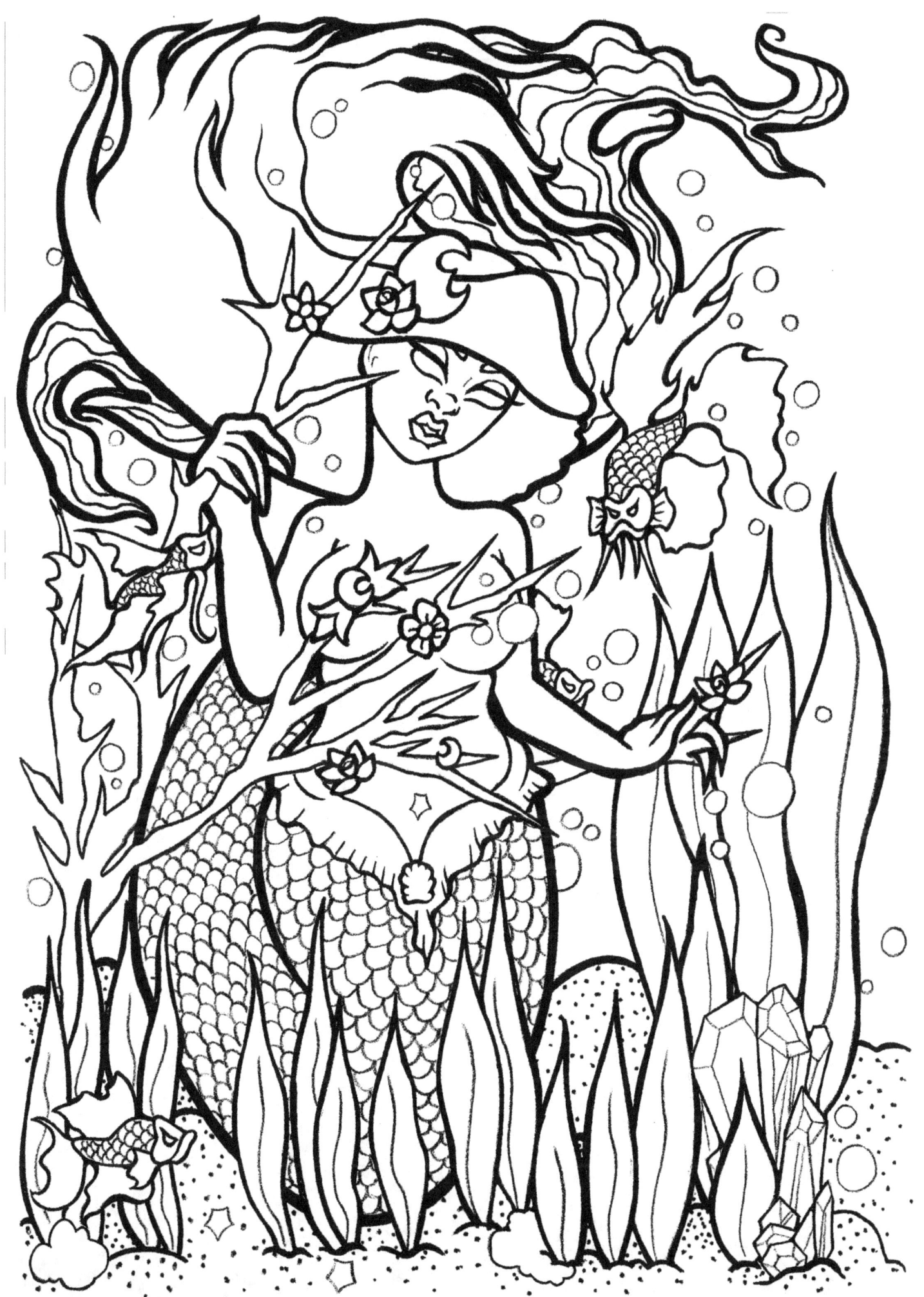

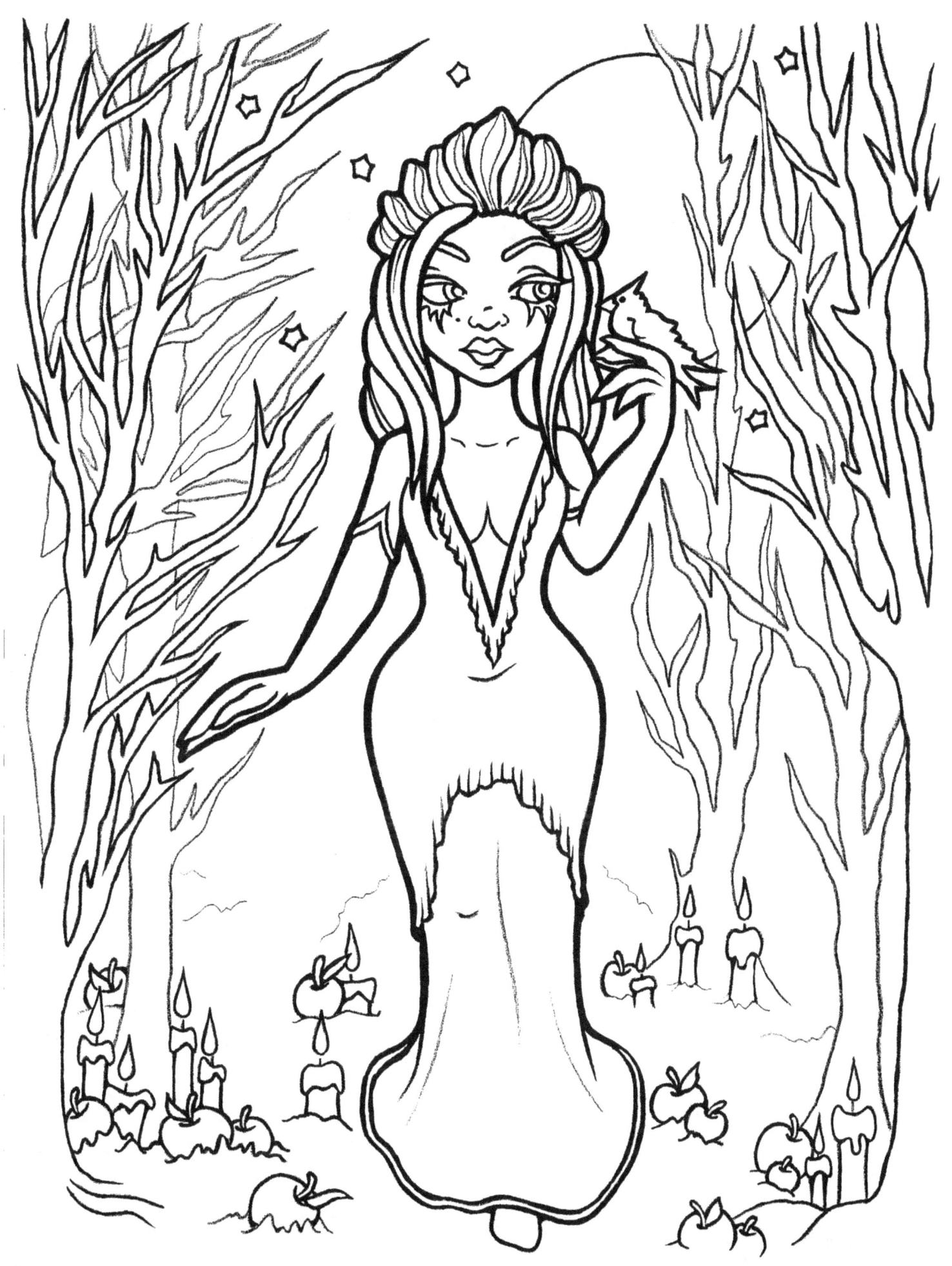

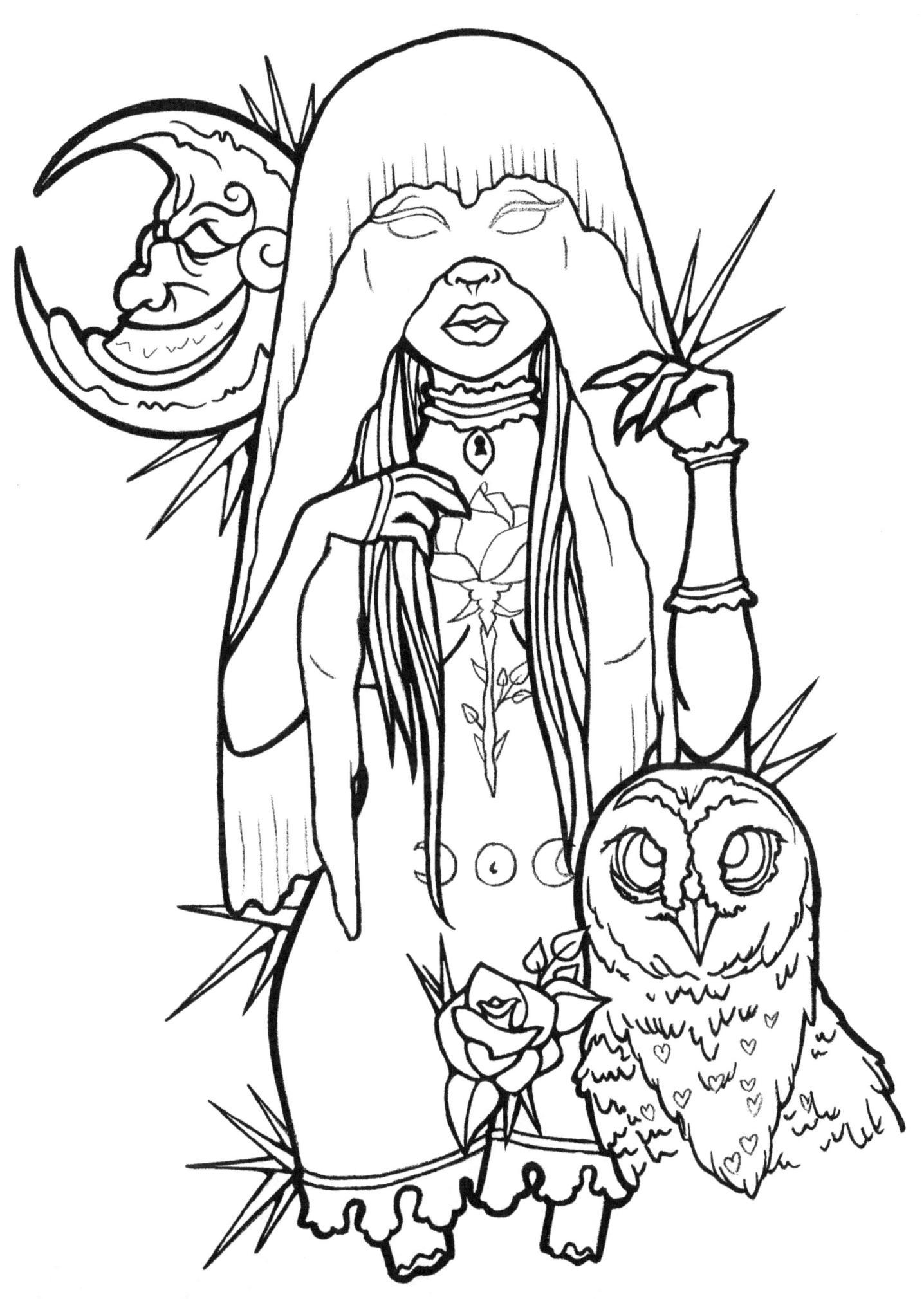

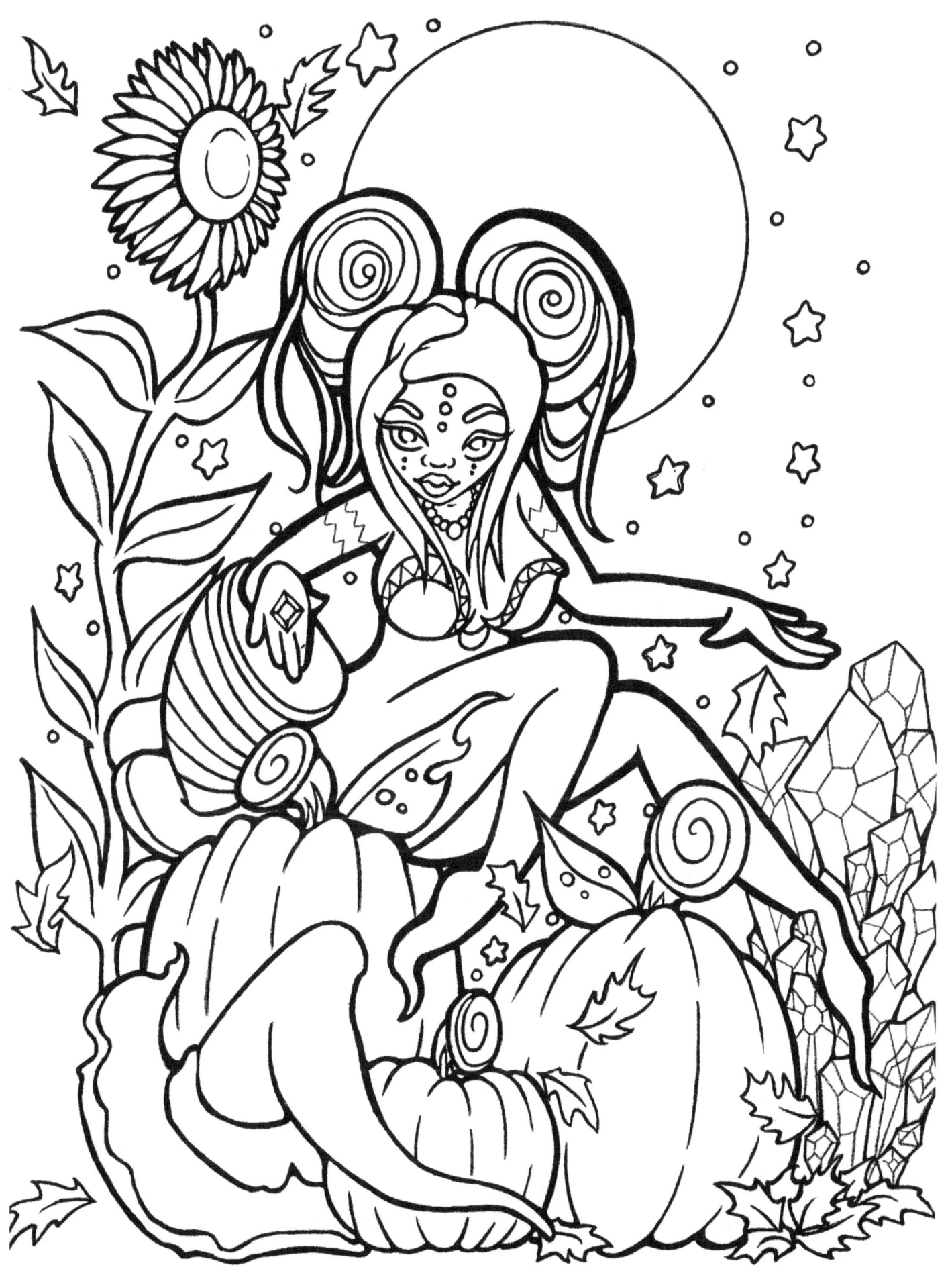

Ms. Muffintop's

Color Test Page!!!

Test your colors here!

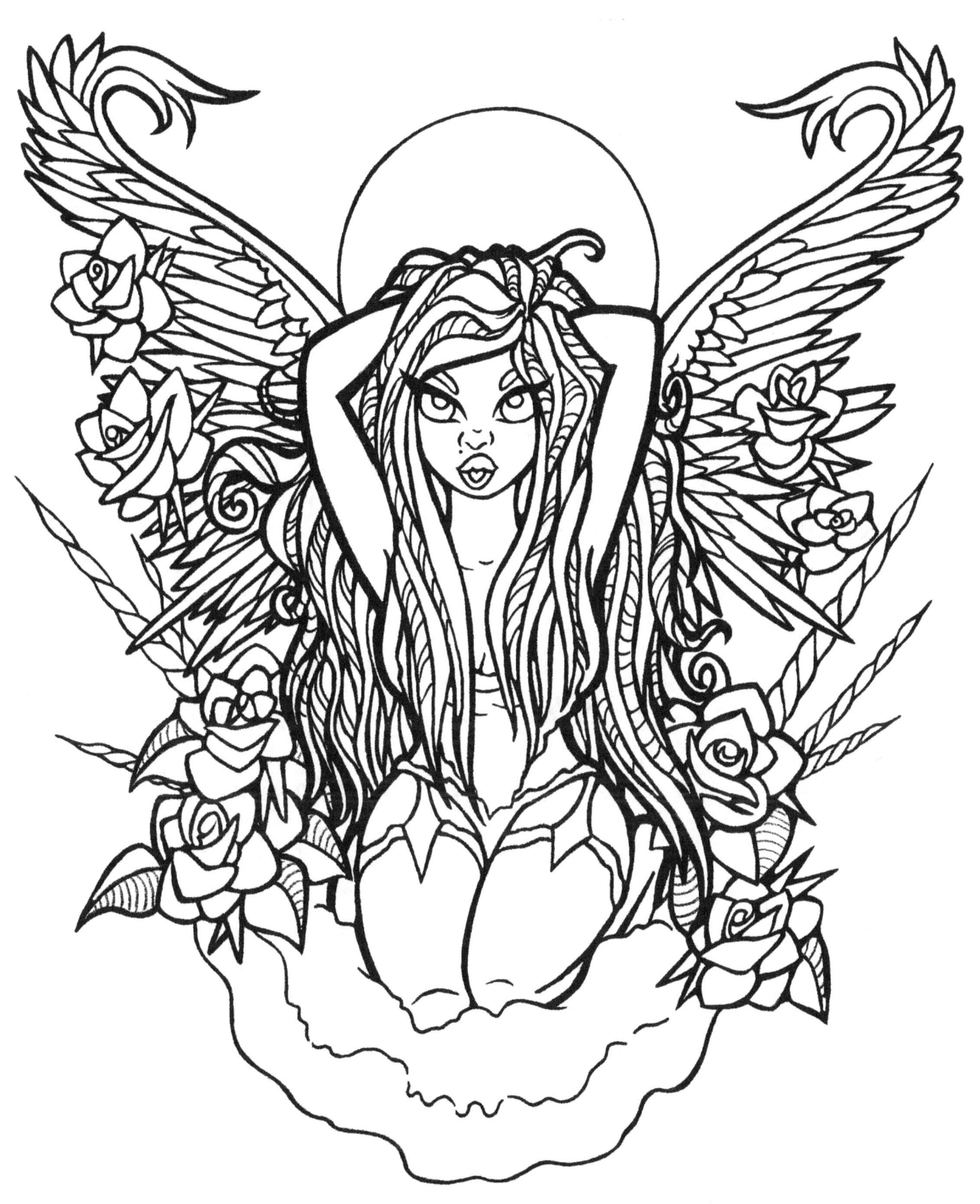

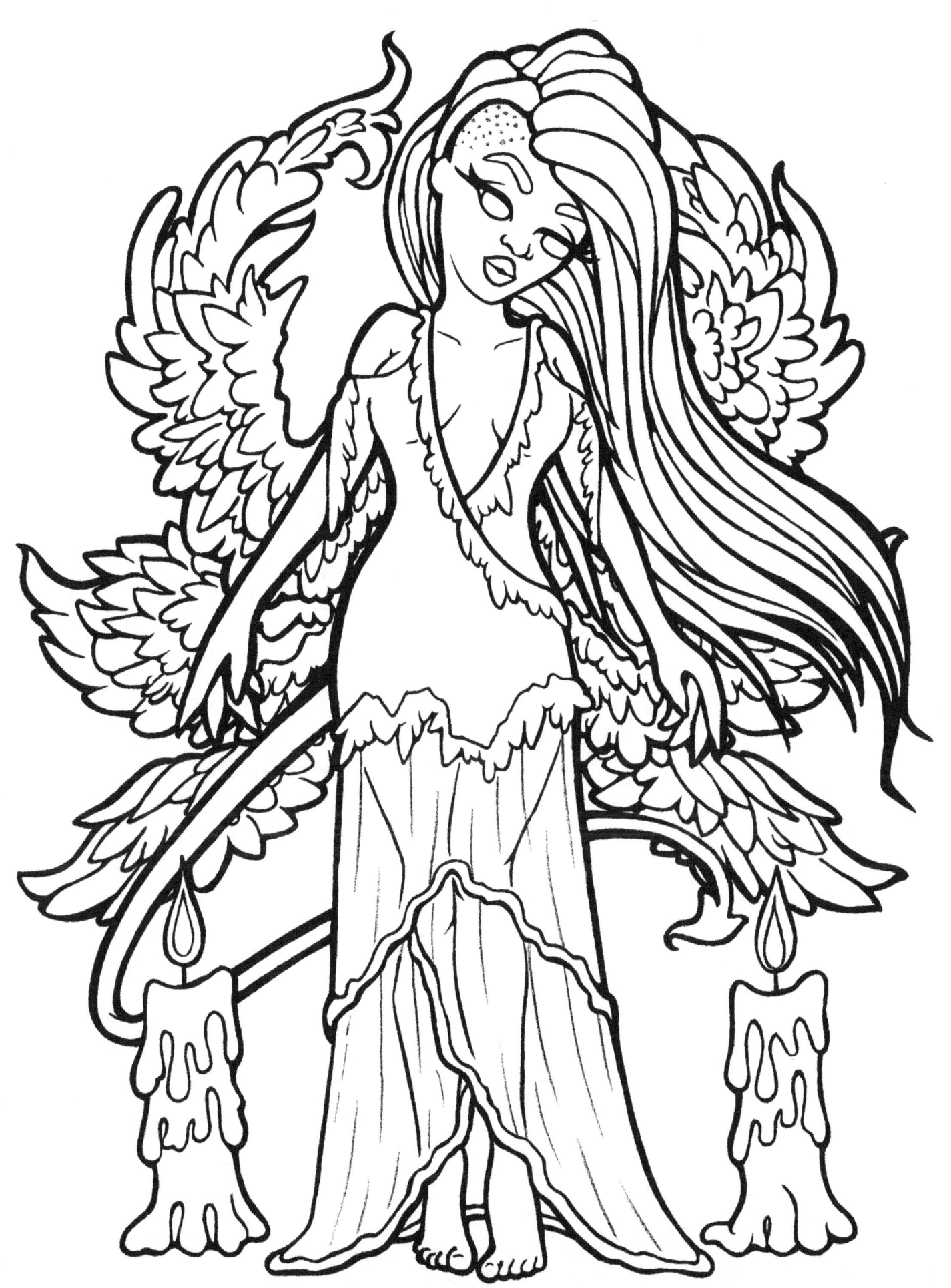

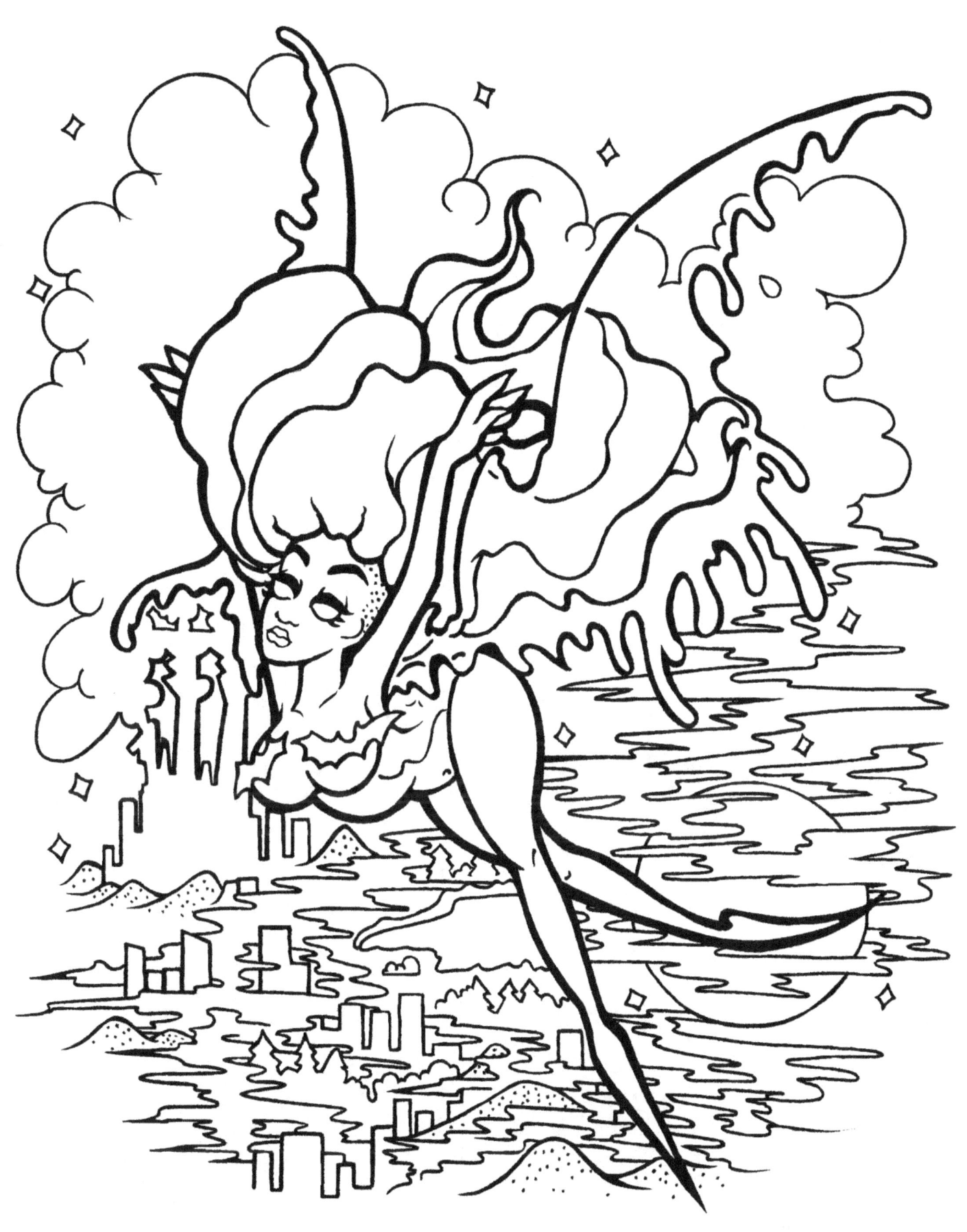

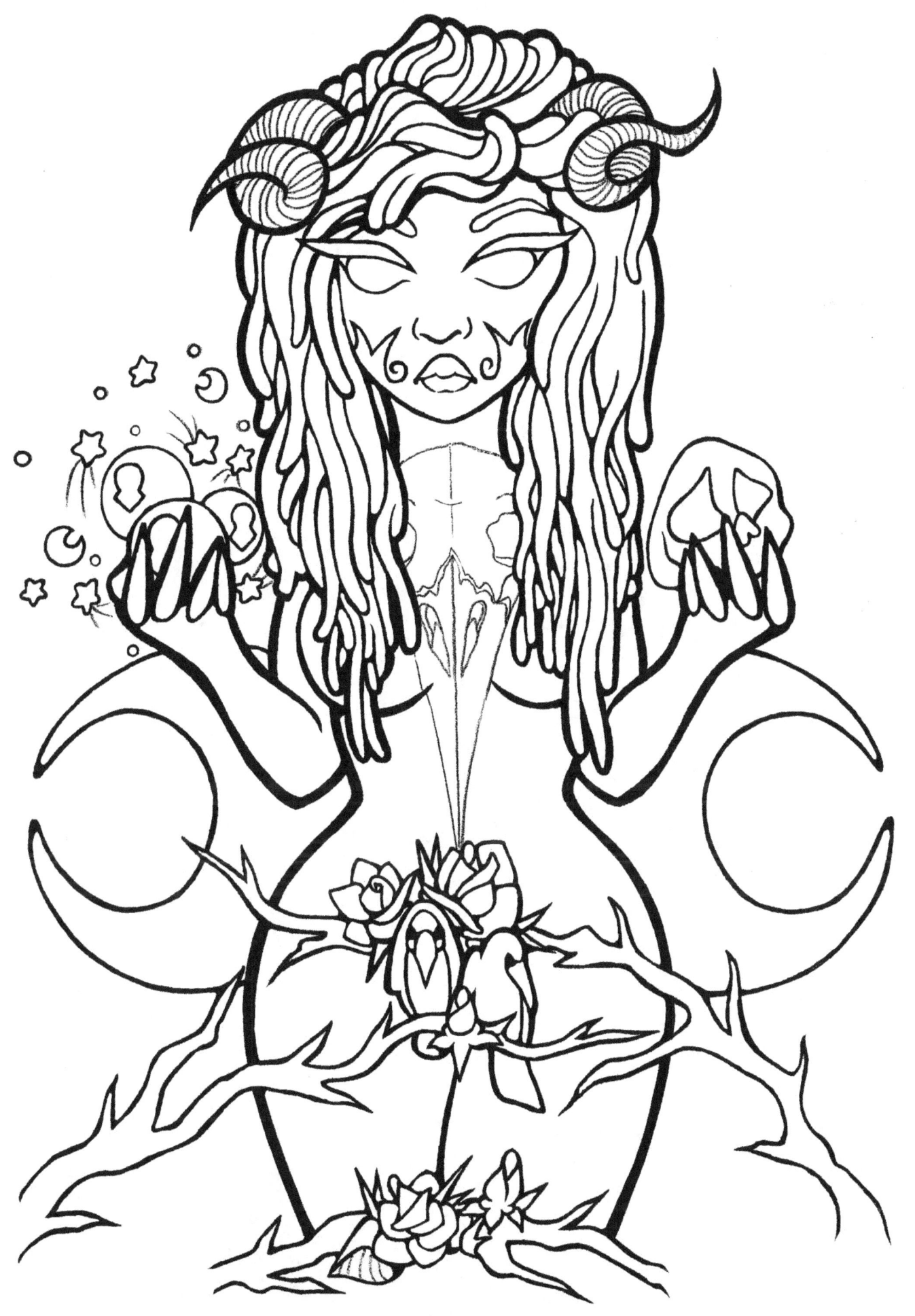

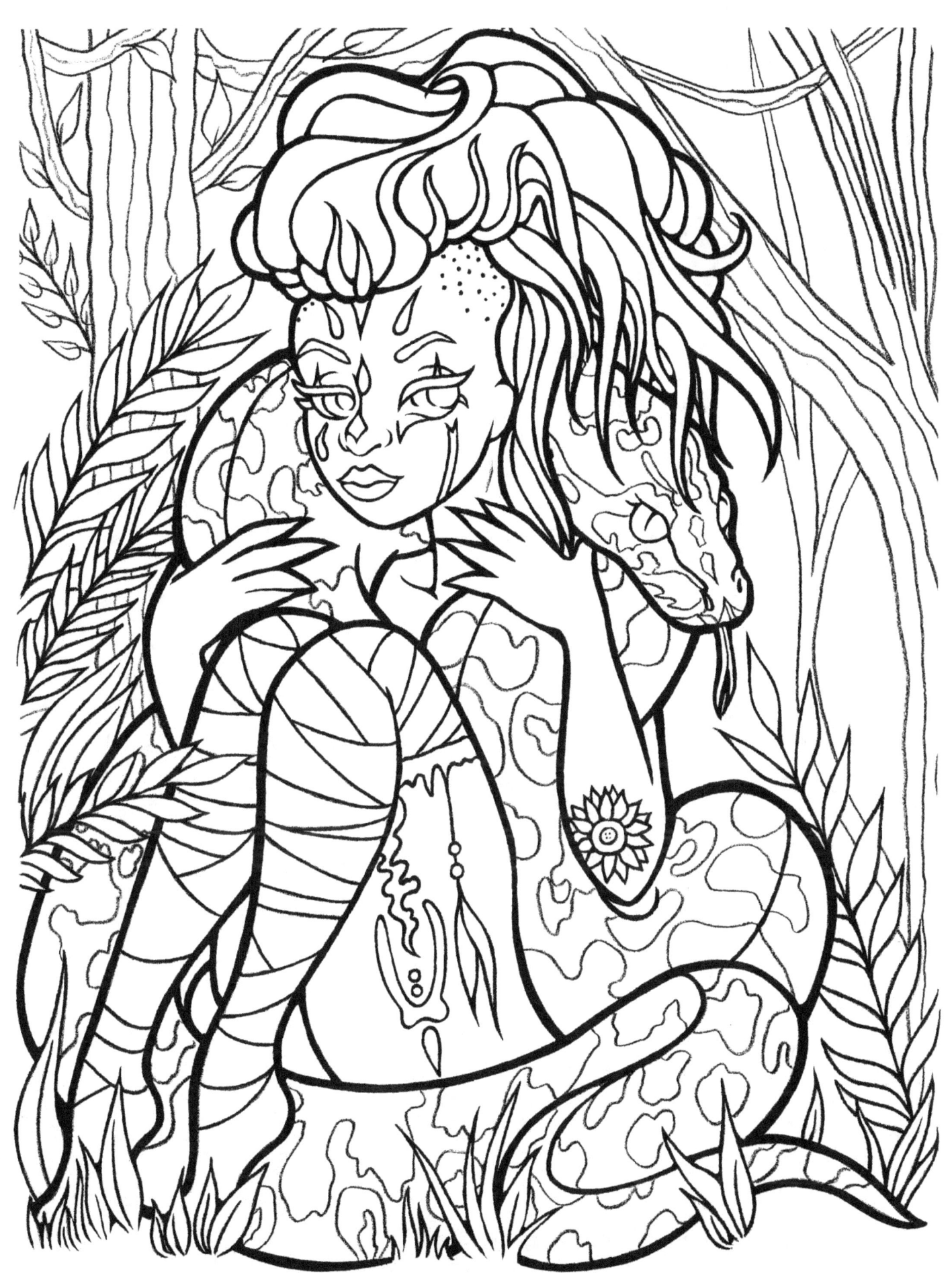

Ms. Muffintop's

Color Test Page!!!

Test your colors here!

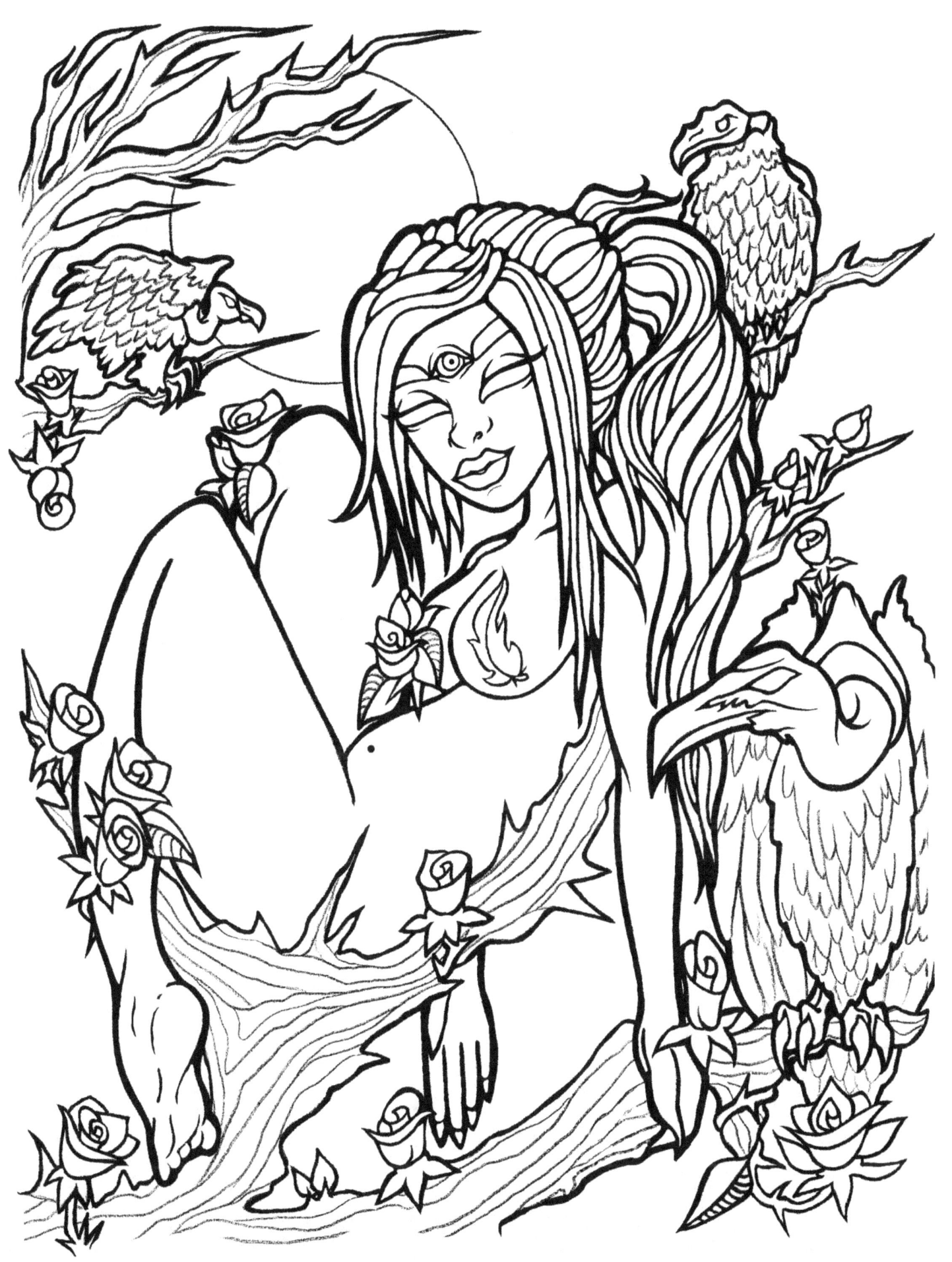

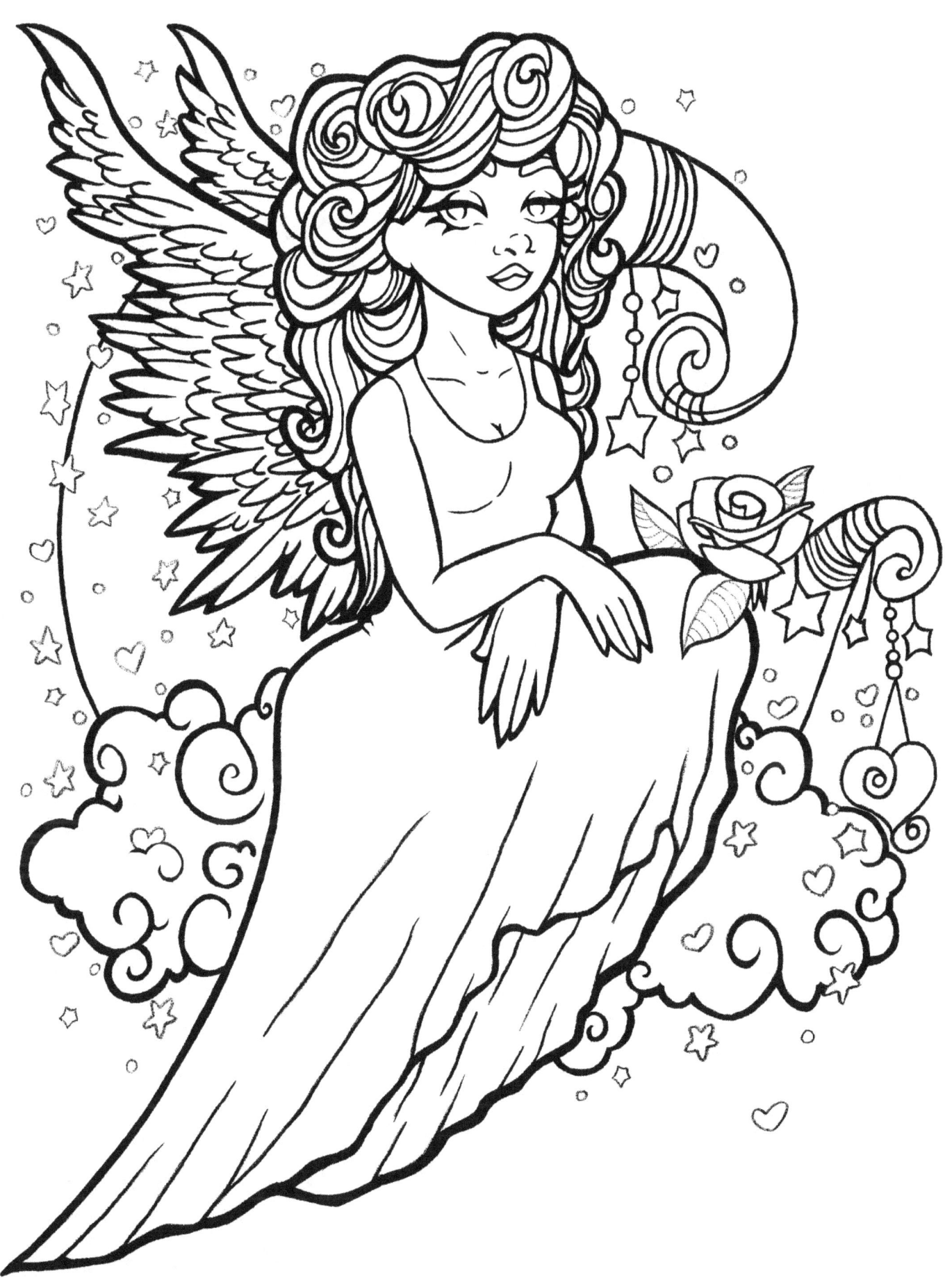

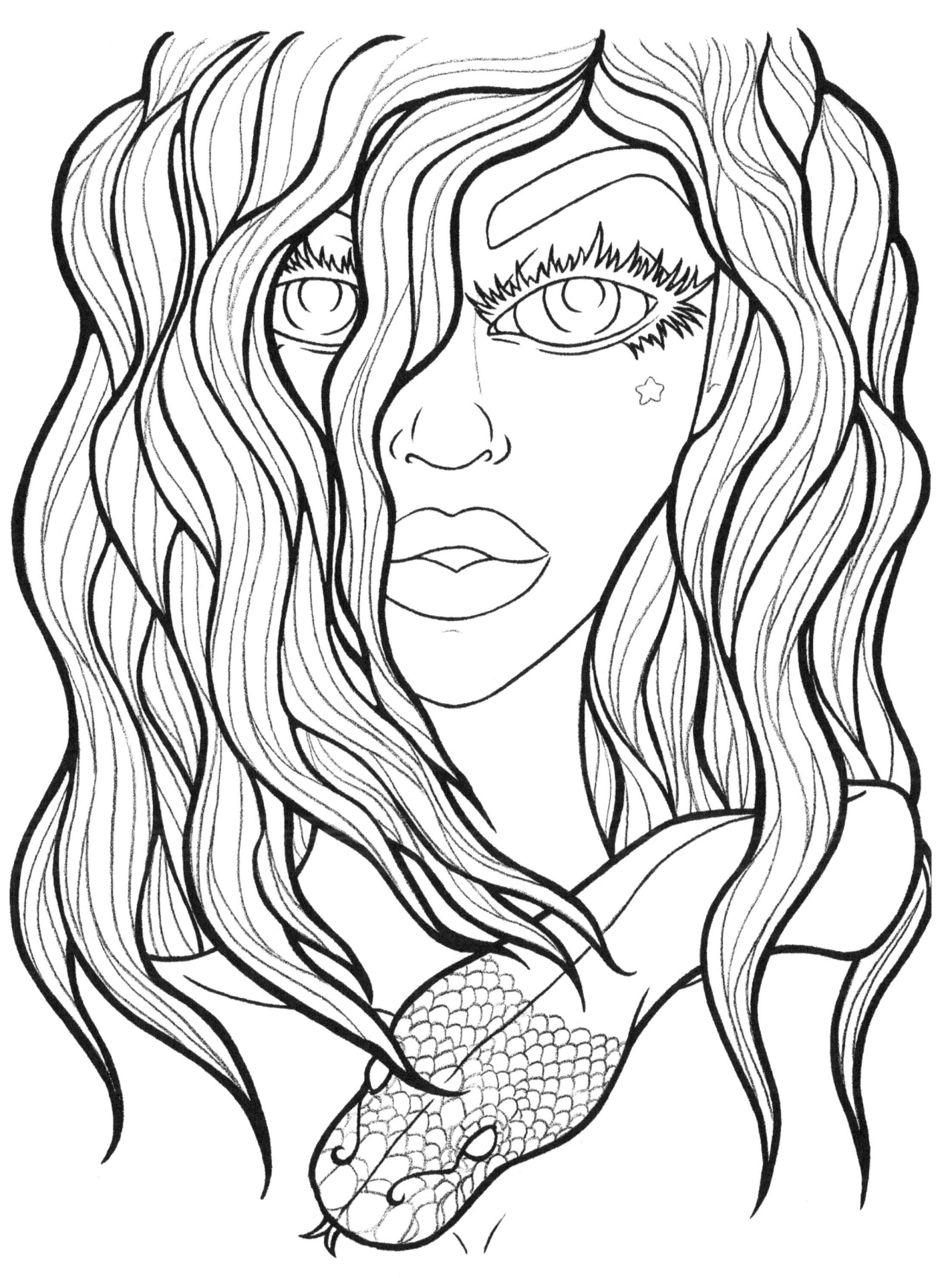

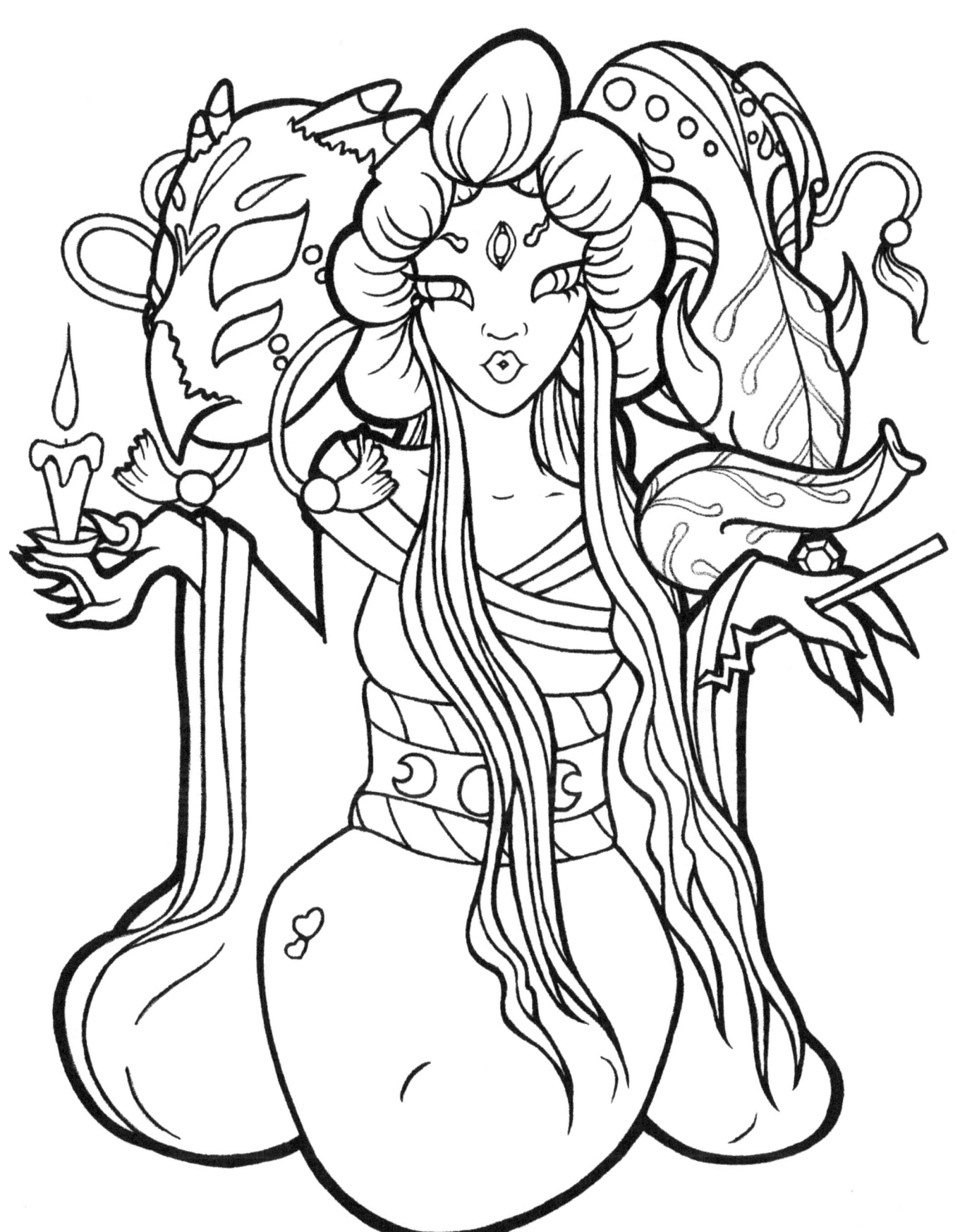

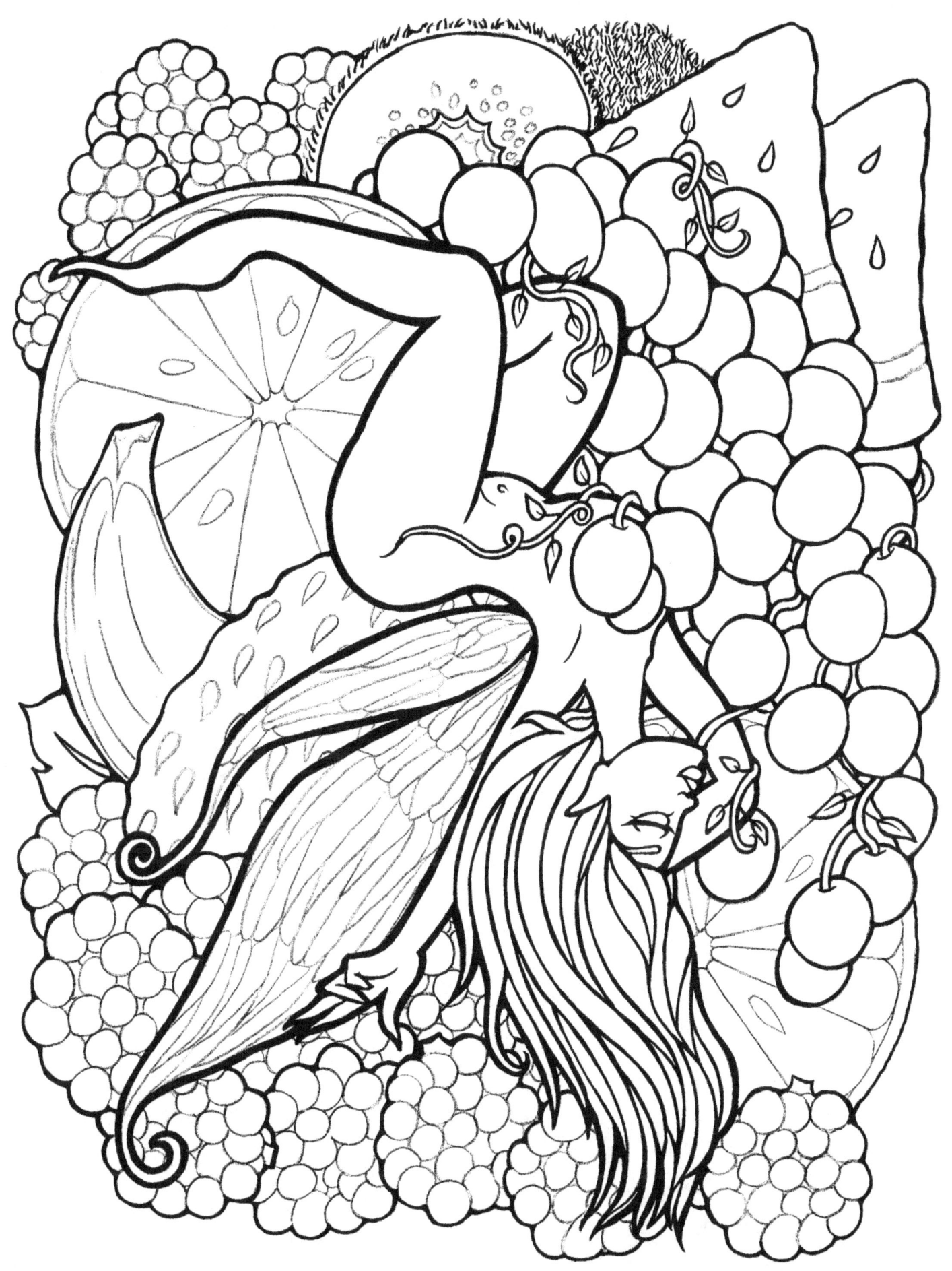

Ms. Muffintop's

Color Test Page!!!

Test your colors here!

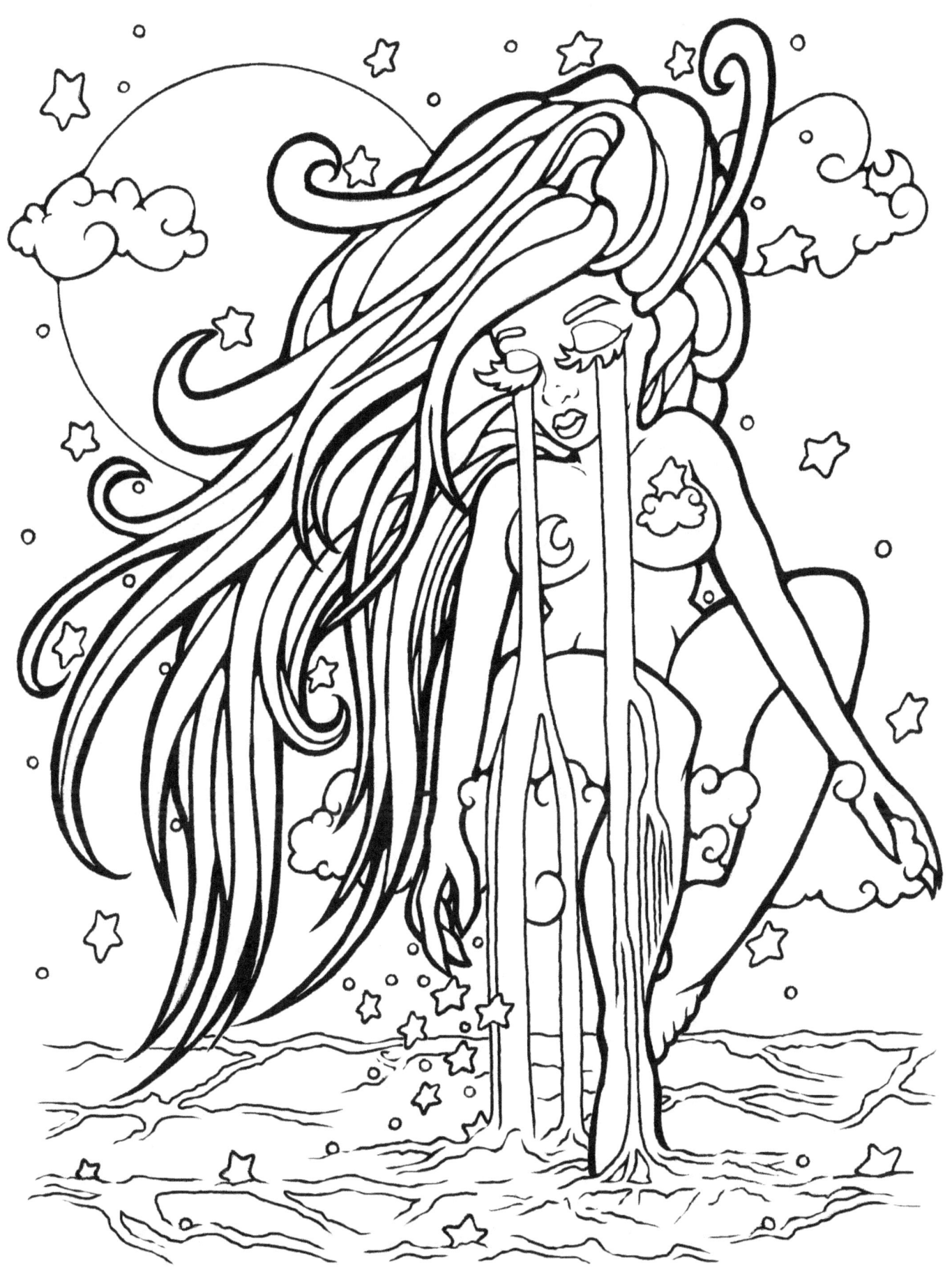

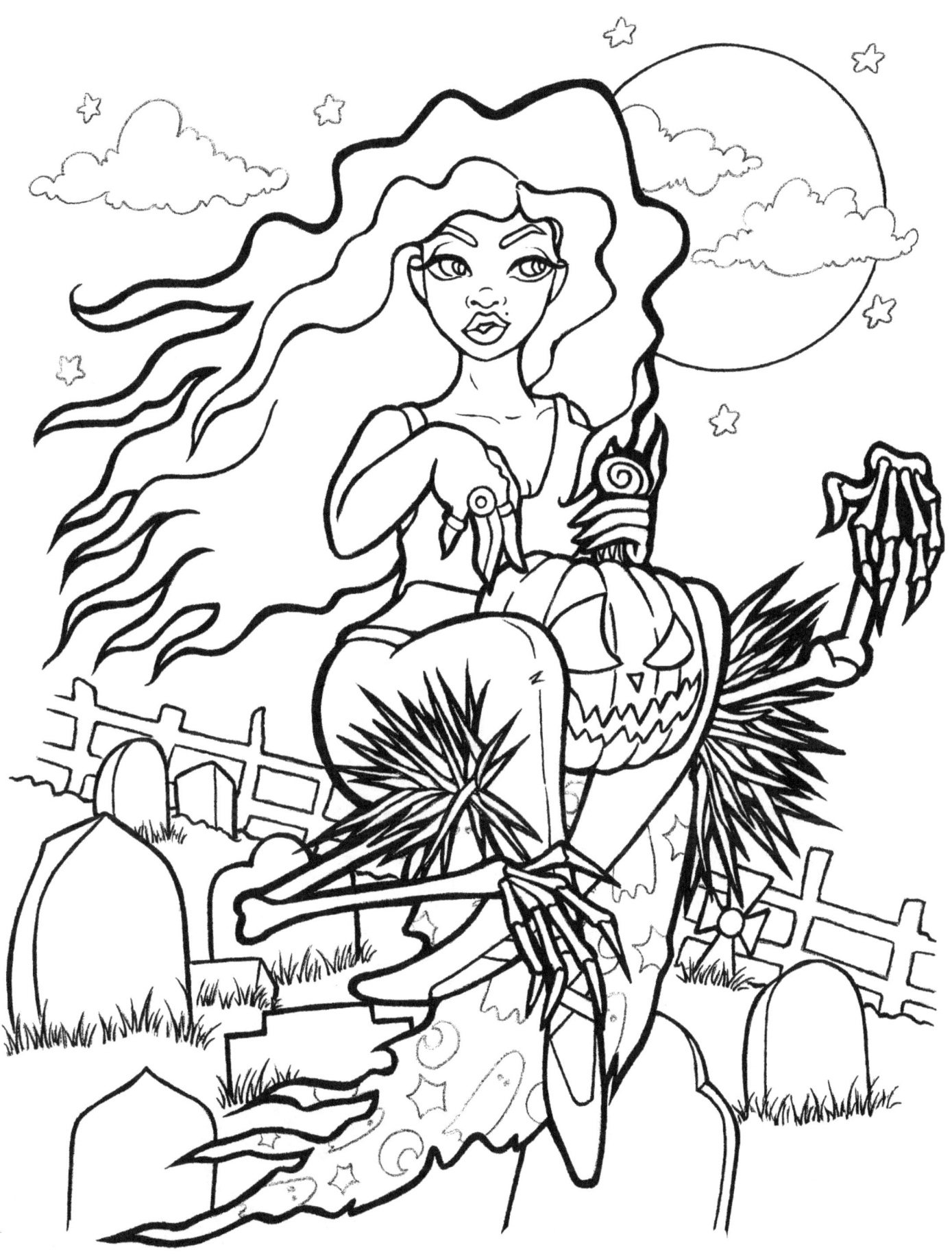

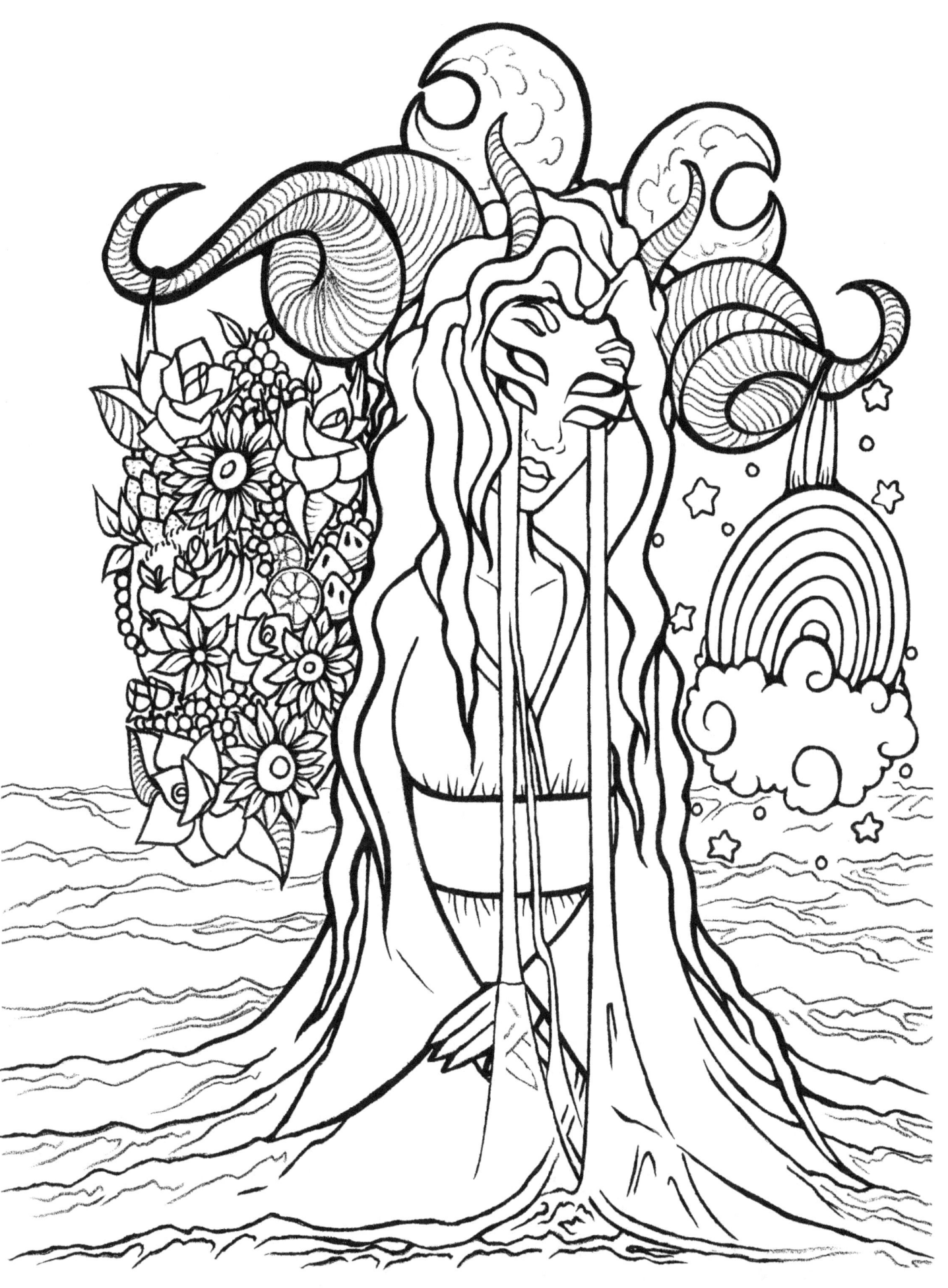

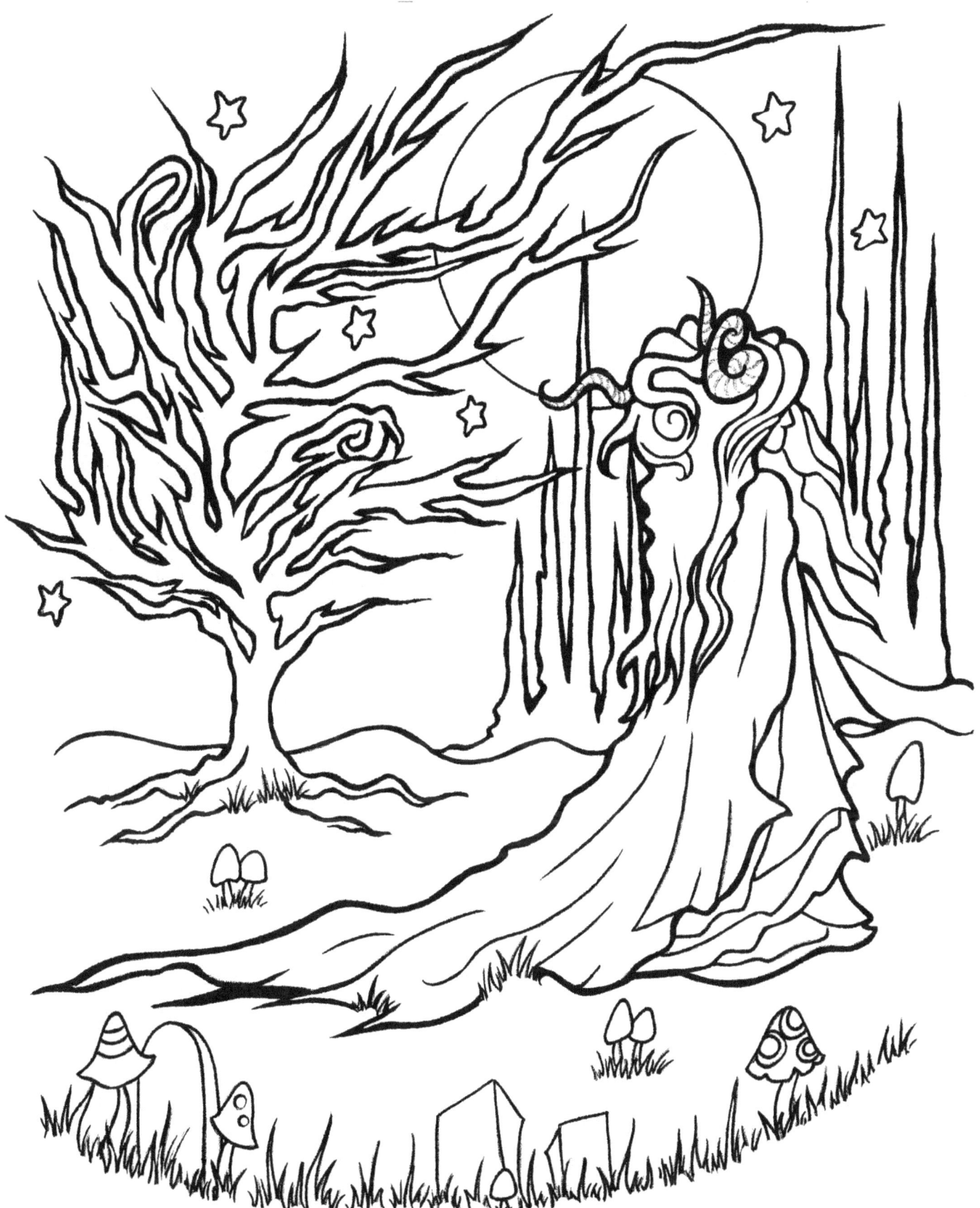

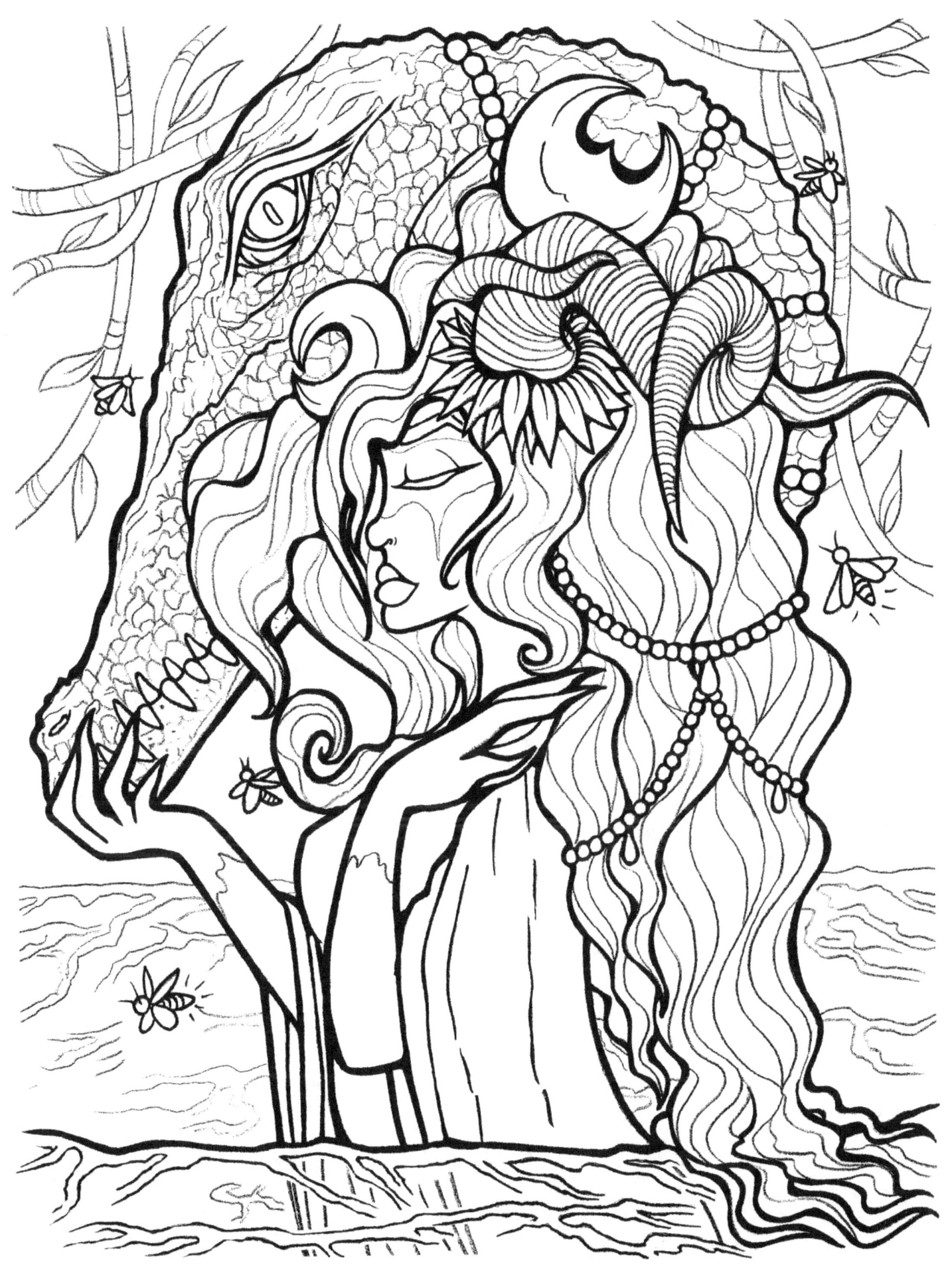

Ms. Muffintop's

Color Test Page!!!

Test your colors here!

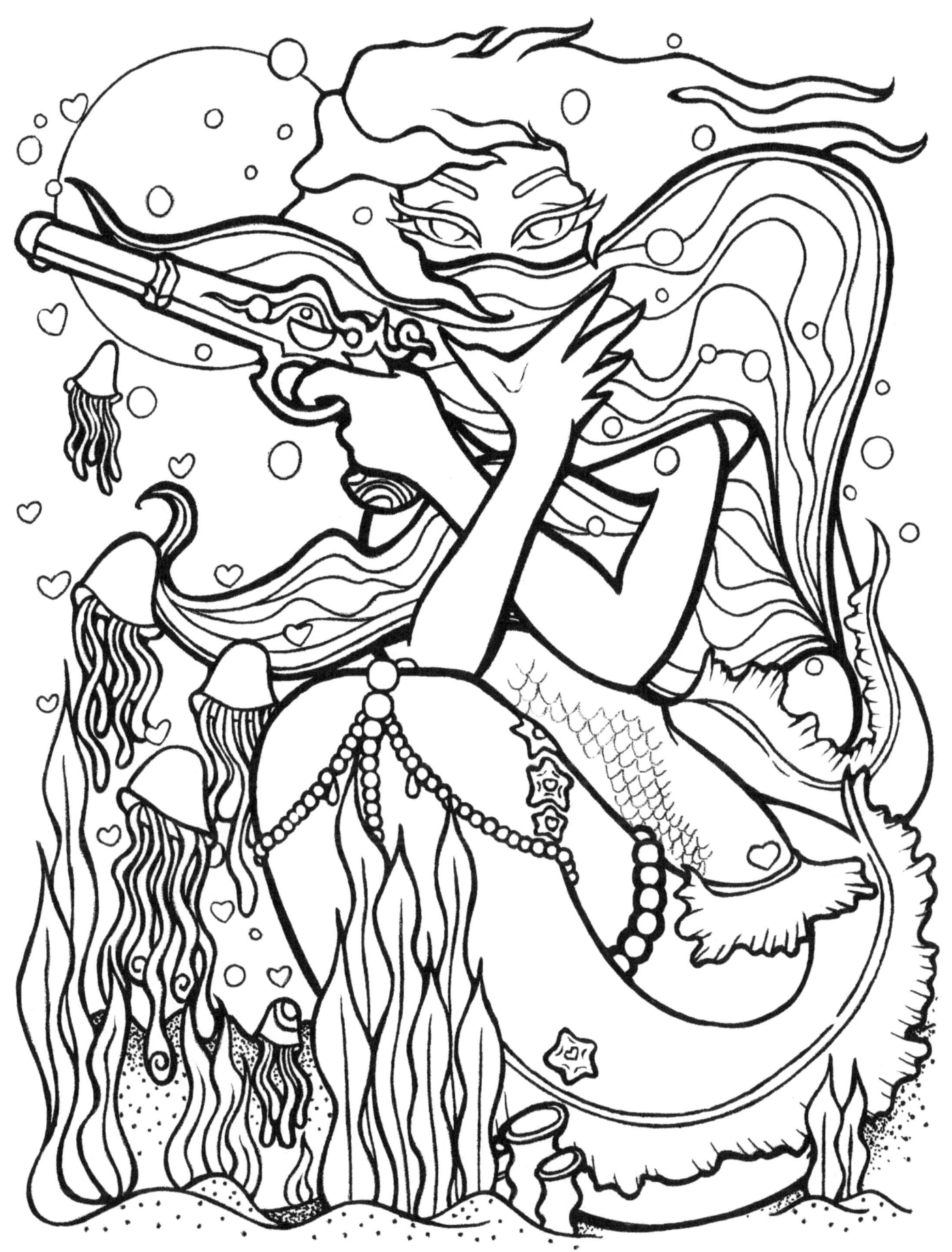

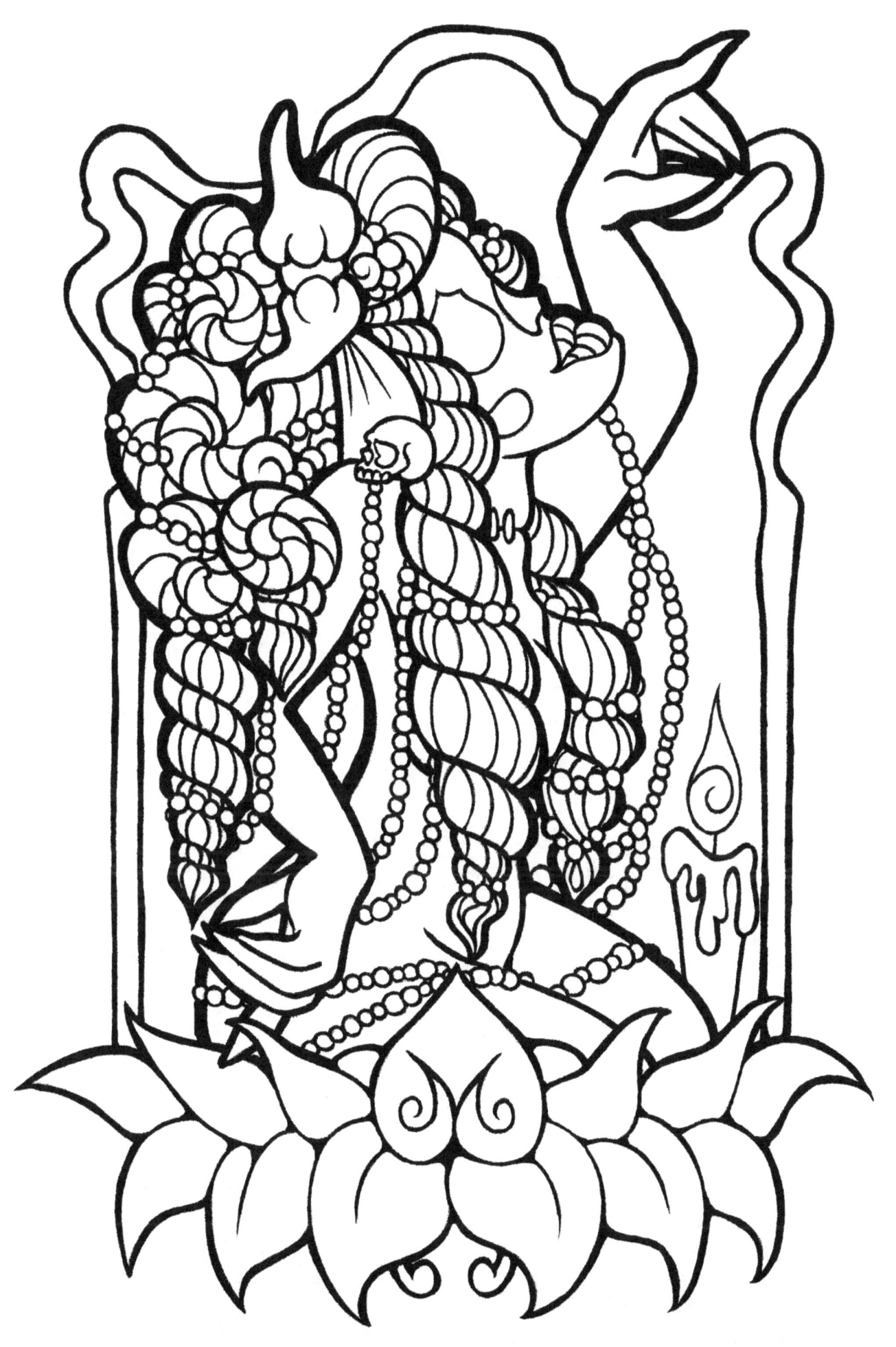

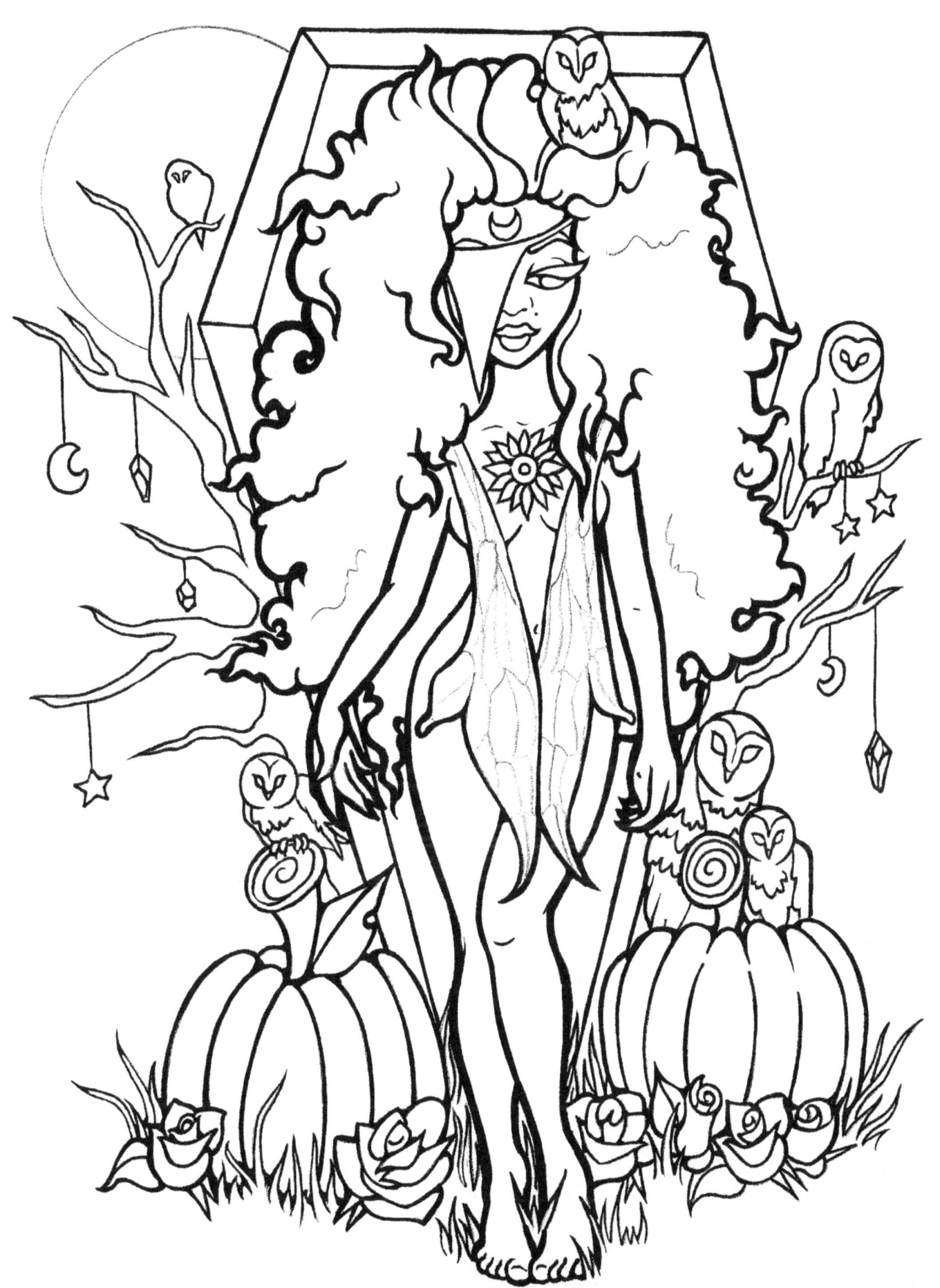

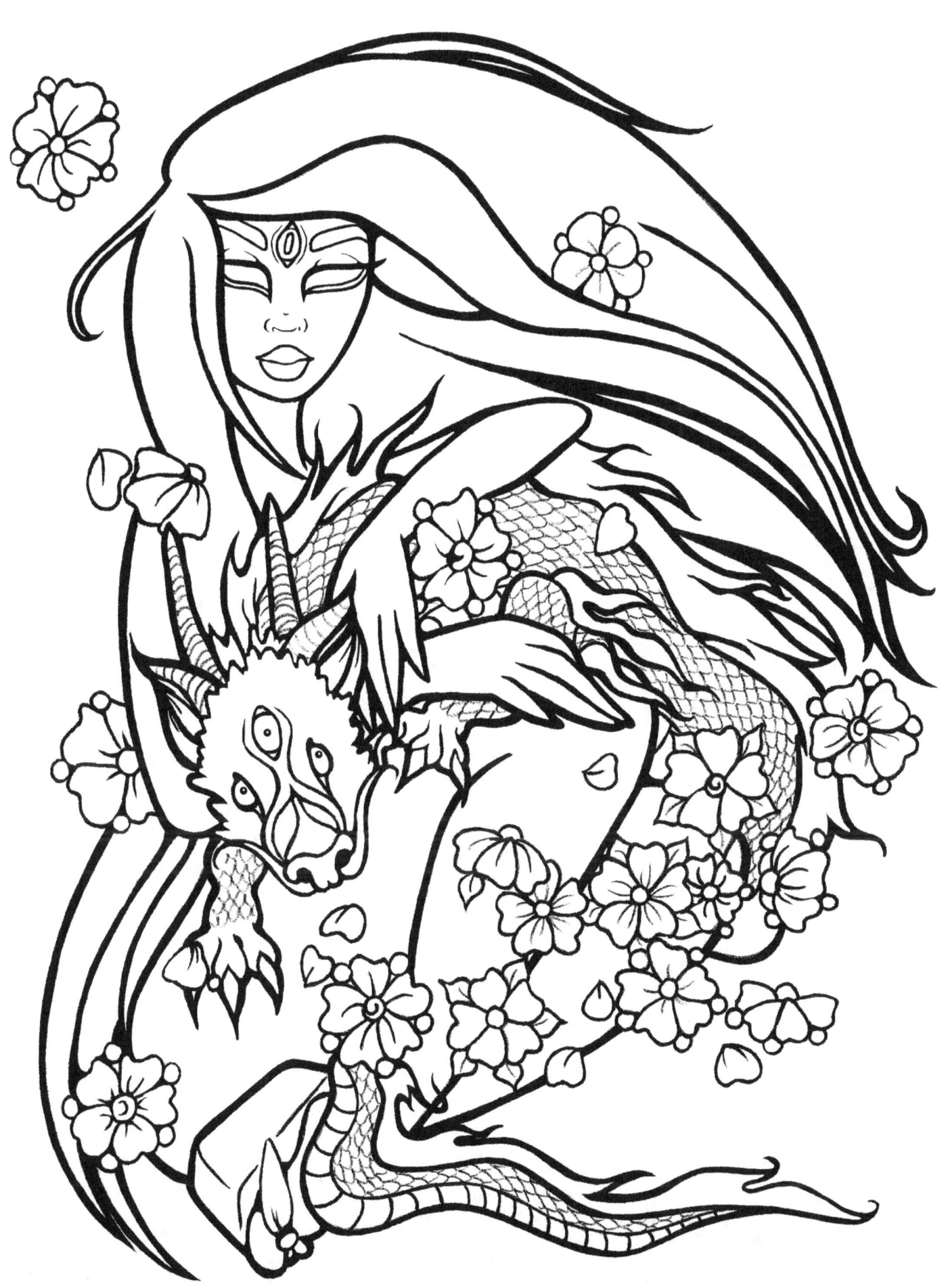

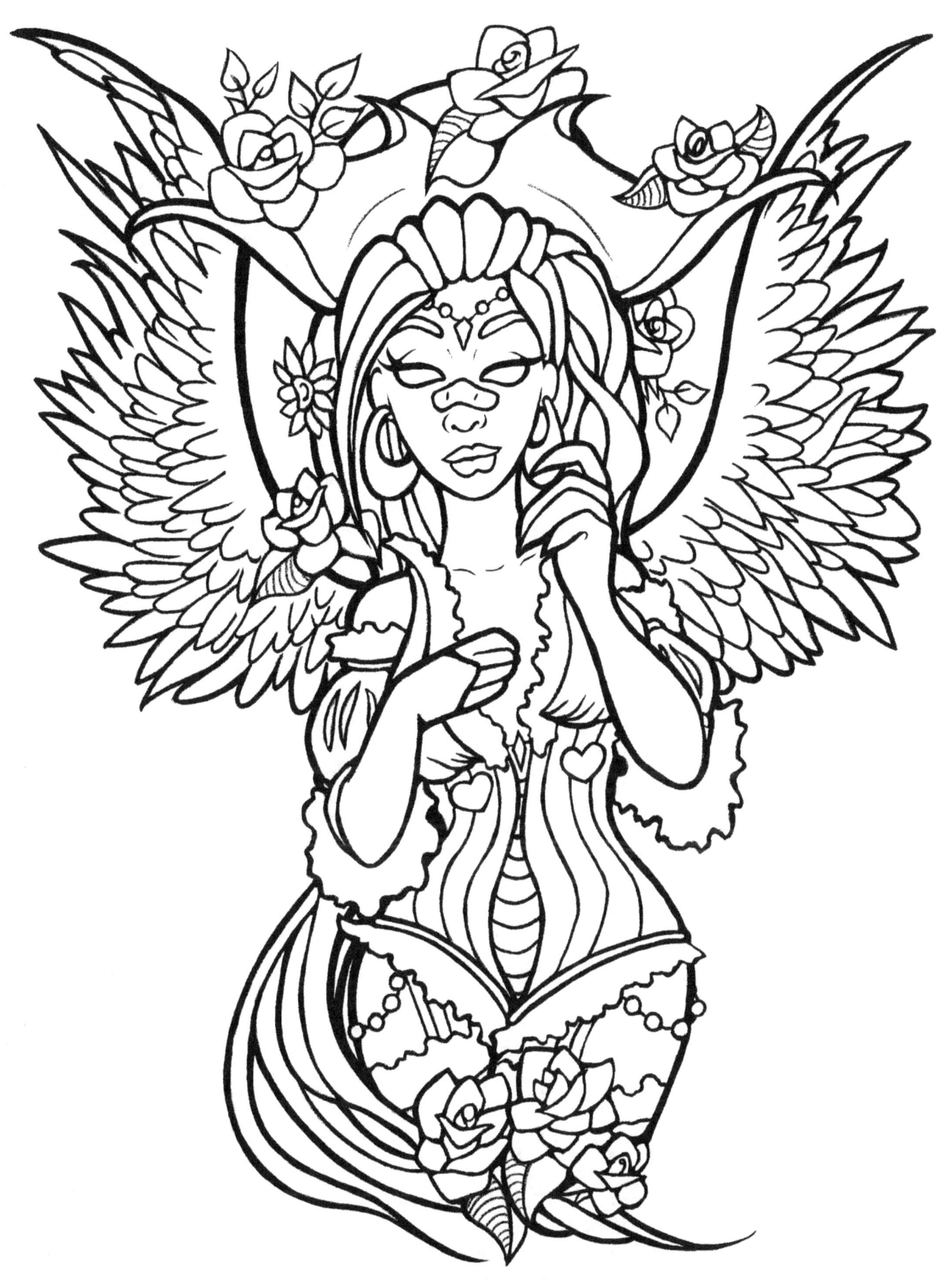

Ms. Muffintop's

Color Test Page!!!

Test your colors here!